Introduction to University Studies

First Edition, Volume 1

Mogana S. Flomo, Jr.

Published by CEPRES International University, 2024.

While every precaution has been taken in the preparation of this book, the publisher assumes no responsibility for errors or omissions, or for damages resulting from the use of the information contained herein.

INTRODUCTION TO UNIVERSITY STUDIES

First edition. January 20, 2024.

ISBN: 979-8223504504

Written by Mogana S. Flomo, Jr..

Table of Contents

Introduction

INTRODUCTION TO UNIVERSITY STUDIES

4.1 Vision for Excellence in Environmental and Public Health Education:

4.1.1 Pinnacle of Academic Distinction:

4.1.2 Interdisciplinary Instruction at all Levels:

4.1.3 Local and International Educational Leadership:

4.1.4 Stimulating Public Health Quality:

4.1.5 Production of Competent and Self-Reliant Graduates:

4.1.6 Global Educational Standards and Best Practices:

4.2 Mission: Stimulating Public Health Quality through Research, Training, and Service Improvement:

4.2.1 Stimulating Public Health Quality:

4.2.2 Through Research, Training, and Service Improvement:

4.2.3 Consultancy and Advocacy:

4.2.4 Premier Standard of Tertiary Education:

4.2.5 Global Educational Standards and Best Practices:

4.3 Goals and Objectives for Providing Premier Tertiary Education:

4.3.1 Providing Premier Tertiary Education:

4.3.2 Producing Competent Graduates:

Course Book description: "Introduction to University Studies at CEPRES International University"

Embark on an enlightening journey into higher education with Dr. Mogana S. Flomo, Jr.'s comprehensive course book. As the founder, Dr. Flomo warmly welcomes learners, emphasizing the pivotal role of understanding CEPRES' history.

Dive into the roots of CEPRES, born out of a response to the 2014 Ebola outbreak. Dr. Flomo's vision transformed a training center into a dynamic university, overcoming challenges with unwavering determination. Explore significant milestones, including the graduation of the first students and hosting an International Environmental Research Conference.

The course book unveils ongoing initiatives at CEPRES, such as training environmental volunteers and active community engagement. Dr. Flomo's vision for the future reflects a commitment to positive change and excellence in environmental and public health education.

Acquire essential academic success skills, from effective study techniques to technological proficiency. Navigate the digital landscape with ease, mastering tools for online collaboration and communication. Engage in reflective practices as you apply learned skills to collaborative final projects.

Beyond academics, the course book weaves a narrative of resilience and determination. Dr. Flomo invites learners into a world where education transforms lives. This isn't just a guide—it's an exploration of growth, knowledge, and success. Welcome to the transformative universe of CEPRES International University.

Welcome and Overview:

WELCOME, STUDENTS, to the intriguing journey of "Introduction to University Studies" at CEPRES International University. I am Dr. Mogana S. Flomo, Jr., and I am delighted to be your guide on this educational adventure.

As we embark on CEPRES101, let me extend my warm greetings to each one of you. This course is not just about academic studies; it is a voyage into the history, mission, and values of CEPRES International University. My aim is not only to equip you with essential academic skills but also to share the remarkable story of how CEPRES came into existence and the challenges overcome to shape it into what it is today.

Picture this: Liberia in the throes of the 2014 Ebola outbreak. The health system strained, and the need for strengthening it became evident. While pursuing my Ph.D. in Public Health at Kwame Nkrumah University of Science and Technology in Ghana, a vision formed – a vision to establish a training center supporting the health system in Liberia. Little did I know that this vision would evolve into CEPRES International University.

In 2015, I legally established the Center for Environmental and Public Health Research (CEPRES). The initial plan was not to start a university but to create a training center collaborating with other Liberian universities. However, faced with skepticism and opposition, I pivoted, deciding to offer certificate and diploma programs directly to students. The dream materialized, and in May 2015, classes began with nearly 200 students.

But every success story has its share of challenges. After the first three months, students started dropping out, and I discovered there was more to it than meets the eye. Undeterred, we persevered, and CEPRES continued to grow. Today, we stand as an institution that has graduated over 500 young Liberians, making significant contributions to environmental and health sciences.

As we delve into this sourcebook, you will gain insights into CEPRES' historical milestones, achievements, and the pivotal role it plays in training environmental volunteers to impact Liberian communities positively. Moreover, we'll explore our current initiatives, future vision, and the groundbreaking ceremony for the official home of CEPRES International University.

This course is not just about academic success skills, computer literacy, and effective communication. It's about understanding the roots of CEPRES, learning from its journey, and being inspired by the vision that led to its establishment. So, let's embark on this educational odyssey together – a journey that goes beyond textbooks and lectures to unveil the story of determination, resilience, and the commitment to building a brighter future through education. Welcome to CEPRES International University, where your academic journey intertwines with a remarkable narrative of growth and impact.

1 CEPRES International University's Formation

1.1 Inception of CEPRES:

LET ME TAKE YOU BACK to the roots of CEPRES International University, a chapter in our story that unfolded during a critical period in Liberia's history – the 2014 Ebola outbreak. As I pursued my Ph.D. in Public Health at the Kwame Nkrumah University of Science and Technology in Ghana, an idea began to take shape, an idea that would soon become the cornerstone of CEPRES.

The devastation caused by the Ebola outbreak exposed the fragility of Liberia's health system. It was during this crisis that the vision for CEPRES was conceived. The original plan was modest – establish a training center that could collaborate with existing Liberian universities to offer programs in environmental and health sciences. Little did I know that this vision would evolve into something much more profound.

The initial idea was simple yet powerful – a center named the Center for Environmental and Public Health Research (CEPRES) that could address the health system's gaps. The strategy was to recruit qualified staff to teach courses, with CEPRES overseeing the process to ensure quality education. The dream was to make a significant impact on Liberia's health sector.

However, as I engaged with university leaders in Liberia, the road ahead proved challenging. The concept of an institution offering courses on behalf of other universities faced skepticism and opposition. The prevailing sentiment was that such an approach was unprecedented and might be impractical.

Faced with this opposition, a crucial decision had to be made. Rather than abandoning the vision, I chose to pivot and take a bold step forward. The vision expanded, and CEPRES transformed from a training center into a fully-fledged university, offering certificate and diploma programs directly to students.

Armed with brochures and flyers, I returned to Liberia in 2015, ready to share the vision of CEPRES with the community. The plan to collaborate with other universities shifted to an independent program rollout, and CEPRES officially commenced classes in May 2015, with nearly 200 students.

This inception of CEPRES was not without its challenges, but it marked the beginning of a transformative journey. This chapter in our story underscores the resilience and adaptability required to turn a vision into reality. As we journey forward, we'll explore how CEPRES navigated challenges, adapted its approach, and emerged as a beacon of education and impact in Liberia.

1.2 Response to the Ebola Outbreak:

NOW, LET ME GUIDE YOU through a pivotal chapter in the story of CEPRES International University – our response to the harrowing Ebola outbreak that swept through Liberia in 2014.

Picture Liberia in the throes of a health crisis, grappling with the devastating effects of the Ebola virus. It was a time of fear, uncertainty, and a glaring realization of the vulnerabilities within the nation's healthcare system.

During my Ph.D. studies in Public Health in Ghana, the impact of the Ebola outbreak in Liberia became starkly apparent. Witnessing the toll it took on the country, I recognized the urgent need to fortify Liberia's health system. The initial vision of CEPRES, conceived as a training center, took on new dimensions in response to the unfolding health emergency.

The outbreak not only exposed the fragility of Liberia's health infrastructure but also served as a catalyst for reevaluating the scope of CEPRES' mission. The focus shifted from merely addressing gaps in the health system to becoming a transformative force that could equip individuals with the skills needed to respond to public health emergencies.

This shift in perspective marked a turning point. The vision expanded beyond offering support to existing universities. It evolved into an institution with a mission to directly impact Liberia's health sector by providing comprehensive education in environmental and health sciences.

The decision to respond to the Ebola outbreak by establishing CEPRES as a university was not just a strategic move but a commitment to addressing a pressing national need. Liberia needed individuals with the knowledge and skills to navigate public health crises effectively, and CEPRES was poised to play a vital role in fulfilling this need.

As we move forward in our narrative, we will explore how this response to the Ebola outbreak shaped the evolution of CEPRES, laying the groundwork for an institution that goes beyond academic excellence to make a lasting impact on the health and well-being of Liberia and its communities.

1.3 Training Center to University Evolution:

LET'S TRAVERSE THE transformative journey that took CEPRES International University from its humble beginnings as a training center to the esteemed institution it is today.

As the initial vision of CEPRES was conceived during my Ph.D. studies in Public Health in Ghana, the primary goal was to establish a training center. The idea was to collaborate with existing Liberian universities, delivering programs in environmental and health sciences to bolster the nation's health system.

However, faced with skepticism and opposition as I engaged with university leaders in Liberia, a critical decision was made. Rather than succumbing to challenges, the vision expanded, and CEPRES underwent a remarkable evolution – from a training center to a fully-fledged university.

The evolution was not just a strategic pivot; it was a response to the dynamic educational landscape and the pressing needs of Liberia. The initial plan of collaborating with other universities shifted to an independent program rollout. This shift allowed CEPRES to directly impact students, offering certificate and diploma programs that aimed to bridge critical gaps in the health and environmental sectors.

The decision to become a university was grounded in the understanding that Liberia needed a comprehensive educational institution that could respond effectively to the challenges posed by public health crises. CEPRES, with its newfound identity, positioned itself as a beacon of academic excellence, ready to address not only immediate challenges but also the long-term educational needs of the country.

The evolution from a training center to a university marked a significant milestone in CEPRES' narrative. It represented a commitment to providing quality education directly to students and, in doing so, making a lasting contribution to Liberia's academic landscape. This transformative journey set the stage for CEPRES to emerge as a key player in shaping the future of education and public health in Liberia. As we continue our narrative, we will delve deeper into the challenges faced, lessons learned, and the indomitable spirit that propelled CEPRES on this transformative path.

1.4 Initial Challenges and Determination:

EMBARKING ON THE JOURNEY to establish CEPRES International University was not without its share of challenges. As the vision expanded from a training center to a full-fledged university, we encountered obstacles that tested our resolve and determination.

Skepticism and Opposition:

- University leaders in Liberia expressed skepticism and opposition to the unconventional model of an institution offering courses on behalf of others.
- The prevailing sentiment questioned the feasibility of such an approach, deeming it unprecedented and potentially impractical.

Determination to Overcome Challenges:

- Faced with skepticism, a crucial decision was made to pivot the vision, transforming CEPRES into an independent university offering certificate and diploma programs directly to students.
- This shift required unwavering determination to navigate the uncharted territory of independent program rollout, challenging traditional educational norms.

Strategies for Gaining Community Support:

- Returning to Liberia in 2015, armed with brochures and flyers, efforts were made to gain community support for CEPRES.
- Outreach initiatives, including radio announcements and community engagement, were implemented to share the vision and goals of the university.

Independent Program Rollout:

- The initial plan to collaborate with other universities shifted to an independent program rollout, necessitating adjustments and strategic shifts in approach.
- CEPRES officially commenced classes in May 2015, marking the beginning of a new chapter in the institution's history.

Launch and Key Personalities Involved:

- The formal launch of CEPRES was a significant event, attended by key personalities such as the County Education Officer of Bong County and Dr. Saaim W. Naamee, the first Chairman of the Board of Trustees for CEPRES.
- Despite challenges, the launch symbolized a collective commitment to the vision and mission of CEPRES.

This phase of initial challenges and determination laid the groundwork for CEPRES to navigate uncertainties and emerge as a pioneering force in Liberian education. The story unfolds with resilience, adaptability, and an unwavering determination to overcome challenges, setting the stage for the institution's continued growth and impact.

1.5 Launch of CEPRES:

THE LAUNCH OF CEPRES International University marked a pivotal moment in the institution's journey, signifying the culmination of efforts, determination, and a bold vision for transformative education in Liberia.

1. *Establishment as a Research Center:*

- In the early stages of development, CEPRES was legally established as the Center for Environmental and Public Health Research in 2015.
- The initial focus was on addressing the health system's shortcomings through research and training.

1. *Focus on Addressing Health System Shortcomings:*

- The inception aimed to contribute significantly to strengthening Liberia's health system by providing education and training in environmental and health sciences.
- The certificate and diploma programs offered were strategically designed to address specific needs within the health sector.

1. *Engaging University Leaders and Community:*

- Efforts were made to engage university leaders in Liberia to garner support for the vision of CEPRES.
- Community outreach initiatives, including radio announcements and distribution of information, played a crucial role in building awareness and support.

1. *Strategic Shifts in Approach:*

- In response to challenges and opposition, strategic shifts were made in the approach, transitioning from the initial plan of collaborating with other universities to an independent program rollout.
- This shift required adaptability and a commitment to ensuring the success of CEPRES as a standalone educational institution.

1. *Launch Event and Key Personalities:*

- The formal launch of CEPRES took place with key personalities in attendance, including the then County Education Officer of Bong County, Mr. Kollieagbo Kapu, Sr., and Dr. Saaim W. Naamee, the first Chairman of the Board of Trustees.
- Despite challenges and initial skepticism, the launch event

symbolized the beginning of a new era for education and public health in Liberia.

The launch of CEPRES not only marked the realization of a dream but also demonstrated the resilience and determination to overcome obstacles. As we delve deeper into the story, we will witness how this launch became a catalyst for growth, impact, and the establishment of CEPRES as a prominent institution in Liberia's educational landscape.

1.6 Engaging University Leaders and Community:

THE JOURNEY OF CEPRES International University involved crucial interactions with both university leaders and the local community. Engaging these stakeholders played a vital role in shaping the trajectory of CEPRES and securing the necessary support for its vision.

1. *Outreach to University Leaders in Liberia:*

- A pivotal phase of the journey involved reaching out to leaders of established universities in Liberia, such as the University of Liberia, Cuttington University, Tubman University, and others.
- The original plan was to collaborate with these universities, offering courses on behalf of them through the Center for Environmental and Public Health Research (CEPRES).

1. *Challenges Faced in Gaining Support:*

- The concept of an institution offering courses on behalf of others faced skepticism and opposition from university leaders.

- The idea of such collaboration was perceived as unconventional and potentially impractical, posing a significant challenge in gaining support.

1. *Strategies for Gaining Community Support:*

- Recognizing the need for community support, extensive outreach initiatives were undertaken.
- Flyers and brochures were distributed, and radio announcements were made to inform the local community about CEPRES, its vision, and the educational opportunities it aimed to provide.

1. *Adjustments in Response to Challenges:*

- Faced with challenges in gaining support from existing universities, strategic adjustments were made in the approach.
- The decision to transition from collaborative programs to independent program rollout marked a significant shift in response to the realities encountered.

1. *Community Engagement and Support:*

- Community engagement efforts were intensified to build awareness and garner support for CEPRES.
- Key personalities from the community, including the then County Education Officer of Bong County, Mr. Kollieagbo Kapu, Sr., played a crucial role in supporting and endorsing the vision of CEPRES.

Engaging both university leaders and the local community was a dynamic and essential aspect of CEPRES' early development. The challenges faced in gaining support prompted strategic adjustments, leading to the independent launch of CEPRES. As the narrative unfolds, we will explore how these engagements shaped the institution's identity and set the stage for its impactful journey in the field of education and public health.

1.7 Strategic Shifts in Approach:

IN THE FACE OF CHALLENGES and opposition, strategic shifts in approach became imperative for CEPRES International University. These shifts marked a critical juncture in the institution's evolution, requiring adaptability and a commitment to ensuring the success of the vision.

1. *Transition to Independent Program Rollout:*

- Faced with skepticism and opposition from university leaders regarding the collaborative model, a pivotal decision was made to transition from offering courses on behalf of other universities to an independent program rollout.
- This strategic shift aimed to establish CEPRES as a standalone educational institution, directly delivering certificate and diploma programs to students.

1. *Adjustments in Response to Challenges:*

- The initial plan of collaborating with existing universities was reconsidered, taking into account the challenges encountered and the need for a more independent and flexible approach.
- Adjustments were made to the organizational strategy, paving the way for a new and innovative educational model.

1. *Focus on Independent Academic Programs:*

- The revised approach involved a focused effort on developing and delivering independent academic programs that aligned with the institution's vision and goals.
- CEPRES began offering certificate and diploma programs directly to students, ensuring a more direct and impactful educational experience.

1. *Strategic Rollout of Certificate and Diploma Programs:*

- The transition to independent program rollout culminated in the official commencement of classes in May 2015.
- Certificate and diploma programs in areas such as water sanitation, hygiene, environmental monitoring, waste management, community health monitoring and evaluation, and project management were strategically rolled out.

1. *Adapting to Changing Circumstances:*

- Adapting to the changing circumstances and opposition, CEPRES showcased resilience and a commitment to its core mission.
- The strategic shifts in approach reflected an agility to navigate challenges and chart a unique path in the educational landscape of Liberia.

These strategic shifts not only showcased adaptability but also laid the foundation for CEPRES to emerge as a pioneering force in Liberian education. The decision to independently roll out academic programs marked a transformative moment, setting the stage for the institution's continued growth, impact, and contribution to the fields of health and environmental sciences.

1.7.1 Launch and Key Personalities Involved:

THE LAUNCH OF CEPRES International University was a momentous occasion that brought together key personalities, stakeholders, and supporters, signaling the official commencement of a visionary educational institution in Liberia.

1.7.2 Formal Launch Event:

- The formal launch of CEPRES took place with great anticipation and enthusiasm, signifying the realization of a dream to contribute significantly to Liberia's education and health sectors.
- The launch event was meticulously organized to mark the beginning of a new chapter in the country's educational landscape.

1.7.3 Attendance of Key Personalities:

- Key personalities, instrumental in the establishment and development of CEPRES, graced the occasion.
- Among the distinguished guests were the then County Education Officer of Bong County, Mr. Kollieagbo Kapu, Sr., and Dr. Saaim W. Naamee, the first Chairman of the Board of Trustees for CEPRES.

1.7.4 Guest Speaker Mr. Kollieagbo Kapu, Sr.:

- Mr. Kollieagbo Kapu, Sr., the then County Education Officer of Bong County, served as the guest speaker for the launch event.
- His presence underscored the significance of CEPRES within the local educational framework, adding an official endorsement to the institution.

1.7.5 Dr. Saaim W. Naamee, Chairman of the Board:

- Dr. Saaim W. Naamee played a pivotal role as the first Chairman of the Board of Trustees for CEPRES.
- His participation in the launch event marked the formal introduction of CEPRES to a broader audience and highlighted the institutional support for its mission.

1.7.6 Recognition of Key Contributors:

- The launch event provided an opportunity to recognize and appreciate the efforts of individuals who played instrumental roles in the establishment and early development of CEPRES.
- Their dedication and commitment were acknowledged as foundational to the institution's journey.

THE LAUNCH OF CEPRES, with the presence of key personalities, was a moment of celebration, acknowledgment, and endorsement. It marked the institution's official entry into Liberia's educational landscape and set the stage for the transformative impact that CEPRES would have on education, public health, and environmental sciences in the years to come.

2 CEPRES Historical Overview and Achievements

2.1 Founding Date and Government Recognition:

THE ESTABLISHMENT OF CEPRES International University is anchored in a specific founding date, coupled with formal recognition by the Government of Liberia, providing a solid foundation for the institution's journey.

2.1.1 Founding Date - November 2014:

- CEPRES International University traces its roots to November 2014, a pivotal period when Dr. Mogana S. Flomo, Jr. initiated the vision and laid the groundwork for the institution.
- The founding date symbolizes the conceptualization and early planning stages that set the institution in motion.

2.1.2 Government Recognition - February 10, 2015:

- A crucial milestone in CEPRES' journey occurred on February 10, 2015, when the Government of Liberia officially recognized the institution.
- This formal recognition marked a significant step in acknowledging CEPRES as a legitimate and authorized entity to operate within the country.

2.1.3 Significance of Government Recognition:

- Government recognition validated CEPRES' commitment to

adhering to educational standards and operating within the legal framework of Liberia.

- The acknowledgment reinforced the institution's standing, contributing to its credibility and authority to confer educational programs.

2.1.4 Foundational Institutional Milestones:

- The period between the founding date and government recognition witnessed foundational milestones crucial for shaping the institution's identity and purpose.
- These early steps laid the groundwork for subsequent developments, reflecting the dedication and vision of Dr. Mogana S. Flomo, Jr.

2.1.5 Impact on CEPRES' Institutional Identity:

- The combination of a specific founding date and government recognition served as cornerstones in shaping CEPRES' institutional identity.
- These milestones provided a solid framework for the institution to grow, evolve, and contribute meaningfully to the educational landscape of Liberia.

AS WE DELVE DEEPER into CEPRES International University's narrative, the founding date and government recognition will continue to play a pivotal role in understanding the institution's inception, growth, and impact on education, public health, and environmental sciences in Liberia.

2.2 Graduation Milestones and International Environmental Research Conference:

CEPRES INTERNATIONAL University's journey is marked not only by its foundational milestones but also by significant academic achievements and its participation in a landmark International Environmental Research Conference.

2.2.1 Graduation of the First 15 Students - February 2016:

- A major achievement for CEPRES occurred in February 2016 with the graduation of the first cohort of students.
- This milestone underscored the successful implementation of academic programs and the culmination of the inaugural phase of the institution's educational initiatives.

2.2.2 Namo Bomosie Environmental Research Conference in Gbarnga - March 2016:

- In March 2016, CEPRES hosted the first Environmental Research Conference in Gbarnga, Bong County.
- The conference brought together national and international guests, including professors from partner universities and representatives from the United Nations Development Programme (UNDP), Liberia.

2.2.3 National and International Collaboration:

- The conference served as a platform for fostering collaboration between CEPRES and national and international entities.
- Engagement with UNDP and professors from partner universities showcased CEPRES' commitment to creating a

global network in education, public health, and environmental research.

2.2.4 Showcasing Research Contributions:

- The Namo Bomosie Environmental Research Conference provided a venue for CEPRES to showcase its research contributions and advancements in environmental and public health sciences.
- It served as a forum for sharing insights, fostering academic dialogue, and contributing to the broader discourse on critical issues in the field.

2.2.5 Highlighting Institutional Growth:

- Both the graduation of the first 15 students and the hosting of the International Environmental Research Conference highlighted CEPRES' rapid growth and positive impact within a short timeframe.
- These milestones affirmed the institution's commitment to academic excellence and its potential to become a key player in the educational landscape.

AS WE NAVIGATE THROUGH CEPRES International University's narrative, these graduation milestones and the participation in the Namo Bomosie Environmental Research Conference represent pivotal moments in the institution's journey, showcasing its commitment to academic excellence and its growing influence on national and international platforms.

3 Current Initiatives and Future Vision

3.1 Current Programs and Initiatives:

CEPRES INTERNATIONAL University, with its roots firmly planted in the vision of Dr. Mogana S. Flomo, Jr., has evolved to offer diverse programs and initiatives that align with its mission of promoting excellence in environmental and public health education. Here is an overview of the current programs and initiatives:

3.1.1 Ongoing Programs and Initiatives:

AT THE HEART OF CEPRES International University's commitment lies an array of dynamic academic programs designed to equip students with profound knowledge and skills in Agriculture, Education, Engineering, environmental and health sciences, etc. These ongoing initiatives not only cater to the evolving needs of students but also reflect the institution's unwavering commitment to staying relevant and impactful in the academic landscape.

The university's dedication to academic excellence extends beyond traditional teaching methods. Notably, CEPRES boasts its project/problem-based learning approach and the establishment of the CEPRES Journal of Science and Innovation Studies (CEJSIS). This groundbreaking initiative serves as a platform for experts and students alike to contribute to the academic discourse.

3.1.1.1 CEPRES Journal of Science and Innovation Studies (CEJSIS): A Proposal

IN A PROPOSAL SUBMITTED to the Founder of CEPRES International University, Assoc Prof. Omobolanle Nosiru outlined the vision for CEJSIS. This scholarly endeavor promotes academic scholarship in various fields, including Health, Physical Education, Recreation & Sports, Physics, Chemistry, Biology, Mathematics, Computer Science, Agriculture Science, Home Economics, and Technology Education.

The objectives of CEJSIS include fostering academic exchange, exposing practitioners to current strategies in teaching and research, and promoting the knowledge, attitude, and skills of students in research and pedagogy. This initiative aligns with CEPRES's broader mission to contribute significantly to the advancement of education in Liberia and beyond.

The contributors to CEJSIS were envisioned to include lecturers, coaches, health professionals, and researchers from CEPRES and beyond, both nationally and internationally.

The editorial team, comprising experienced professionals from Liberia, Ghana, Nigeria, USA, and Southern Africa, ensures a diverse and knowledgeable perspective. The use of ISSN numbers further enhances the journal's credibility and visibility.

In summary, CEPRES International University not only provides cutting-edge academic programs but also pioneers the establishment of a scholarly journal. CEJSIS stands as a testament to the institution's dedication to fostering academic excellence, collaboration, and the dissemination of knowledge.

Figure 1:(*CEPRES Journal of Science and Innovative Studies, n.d.*)

3.1.1.2 CEPRES Journal of Science and Innovation Studies (CEJSIS):

FOLLOWING THE SUCCESSFUL proposal submission and subsequent approval, the CEPRES Journal of Science and Innovation Studies (CEJSIS) has evolved into a thriving academic venture. This scholarly initiative, initiated by Assoc Prof. Omobolanle Nosiru and endorsed by the Founder of CEPRES International University, has demonstrated significant impact with the publication of two volumes.

Volume 1: March Edition

The inaugural edition of CEJSIS, released in March, marked a monumental achievement for CEPRES International University. The journal featured a diverse range of contributions from lecturers, coaches, health professionals, and researchers in various specializations. The publication highlighted original research and perspectives in Health, Physical Education, Recreation & Sports, Physics, Chemistry, Biology, Mathematics, Computer Science, Agriculture Science, Home Economics, and Technology Education.

The positive reception of Volume 1 underscored the demand for a platform that promotes academic scholarship and facilitates the exchange of ideas among practitioners in these fields.

Volume 2: September Edition

Building on the success of the maiden edition, CEJSIS continued its impactful journey with the release of Volume 2 in September. The publication maintained its commitment to providing a platform for professionals nationally and internationally. The journal not only showcased the achievements and advancements within the various disciplines but also contributed to the broader academic discourse.

3.1.1.3 A Platform for Knowledge Exchange

CEJSIS HAS EMERGED as a vital platform for knowledge exchange, bringing together students, experts, practitioners, and researchers. The diversity of contributors and the multidisciplinary nature of the published works have enhanced the journal's standing in the academic community.

3.1.1.4 Sustained Publication and Future Prospects

WITH TWO VOLUMES ALREADY published, CEJSIS has demonstrated its sustainability. The proposed budget, centered on a self-sustaining model, has proven effective in covering production costs through reasonable publication and assessment fees.

As CEJSIS looks towards the future, there is anticipation for continued growth, expanded readership, and further contributions from the academic community. The journal's success reflects not only the dedication of its editorial team but also the broader commitment of CEPRES International University to advancing academic scholarship and fostering innovation in various fields.

◈ **Expansion Plans and Future Vision:**

As the sun sets on the horizon of academia, CEPRES International University embarks on a visionary journey, setting its sights on expanding program offerings to address the dynamic landscape of environmental and public health. The institution's strategic planning, with an unwavering commitment to societal well-being, includes a pioneering move into vocational education alongside its academic programs.

3.1.2.1 Background and Context of Vocational Training at CEPRES International University

IN RECOGNIZING THE evolving educational needs of its community, CEPRES International University has responded with a comprehensive approach. The establishment of The Institute of Professional Studies signifies the institution's dedication to providing practical learning opportunities. This move is underpinned by a profound educational vision that extends beyond academic and theoretical realms, placing a strong emphasis on practical skills and real-world applicability.

The introduction of vocational training aligns seamlessly with the university's commitment to excellence in education. This commitment extends to bridging the gap between traditional academic programs and the practical skills demanded by industries in the 21st century.

3.1.2.2 Changing Workforce Demands and Addressing Diverse Educational Backgrounds

IN A WORLD WHERE THE job market is evolving rapidly, CEPRES International University acknowledges the importance of equipping students with a diverse skill set. Vocational training becomes the bridge between academic qualifications and the practical skills sought by employers. Furthermore, the university recognizes the diverse educational backgrounds of its community, ensuring that vocational training programs cater to a wide range of learners.

3.1.2.3 Community Development and Integration with Academic Programs

CEPRES INTERNATIONAL University's commitment to community development is palpable. By offering vocational training programs, the institution aims to contribute to the socioeconomic development of the local community. These programs empower individuals with practical skills, enhancing employability and fostering entrepreneurship.

The integration of vocational skills with academic programs at CEPRES International University goes beyond providing a well-rounded education; it offers students a competitive edge in the job market. The synergy between academic knowledge and practical skills is a strategic response to the evolving needs of students and employers.

3.1.2.4 National and Global Trends

THE DECISION TO INTRODUCE vocational training aligns with national and global trends in education. Recognizing the importance of vocational education in addressing workforce needs and reducing unemployment rates, CEPRES International University positions itself as a contributor to the overall development of the educational landscape.

3.1.2.5 Objectives of the Program

THE VOCATIONAL TRAINING programs at CEPRES International University are crafted with clear and well-defined objectives:

1. ***Empowerment and Skill Development***: To equip individuals with practical skills applicable in various industries, fostering a deep understanding of chosen fields.
2. ***Enhanced Employability***: To enhance participants' employability by providing industry-relevant skills, reducing unemployment in the community.
3. ***Entrepreneurship Development***: To nurture entrepreneurial spirit and provide the knowledge required for starting and managing businesses.
4. ***Diversity and Inclusivity***: To offer inclusive educational opportunities for individuals with diverse educational backgrounds.
5. ***Alignment with Industry Needs***: To ensure the curriculum meets current and emerging needs, bridging the gap between academia and industry.
6. ***Integration with Academic Programs***: To seamlessly integrate vocational skills with academic studies for a well-rounded education.
7. ***Community Development***: To contribute to the overall development of the local community by creating a skilled workforce.
8. ***Evaluation and Improvement***: To continually assess and improve programs based on changing educational and industry requirements.
9. ***Global Competitiveness***: To prepare students to compete globally by providing skills that transcend local job markets.
10. ***Quality Assurance:*** To maintain high standards of quality, meeting or exceeding industry and educational benchmarks.

In conclusion, the introduction of vocational training programs at CEPRES International University reflects a strategic commitment to holistic education. These programs embody empowerment, employability, entrepreneurship, inclusivity, industry relevance, community development, global competitiveness, and quality assurance. Together, these objectives contribute to the university's mission of providing a well-rounded and practical education for its students.

3.1.3 Graduation of Environmental Volunteers and Their Impact:

CEPRES INTERNATIONAL University, in its unwavering dedication to community engagement and the practical application of knowledge, undertook a notable initiative – the training of Environmental Volunteers. This program stands as a testament to the institution's commitment to creating a positive impact beyond academic boundaries.

3.1.3.1 Role of Environmental Volunteers

Figure 2: Photos selected from Environmental volunteer graduation program

GRADUATES OF THE ENVIRONMENTAL Volunteers program emerge as ambassadors of change, poised to redirect the focus of young people toward pressing environmental issues. Armed with knowledge and practical skills, these volunteers become catalysts for promoting health, cleanliness, and safety in Liberian cities.

3.1.3.2 Demonstrating Commitment to Environmental Stewardship

THE INITIATIVE TO TRAIN Environmental Volunteers aligns seamlessly with CEPRES International University's commitment to environmental stewardship. By imparting knowledge and instilling a sense of responsibility, the university contributes to building a cadre of individuals dedicated to the well-being of their communities and the environment.

3.1.3.3 Promoting Health and Safety

THE IMPACT OF THESE graduates extends far beyond theoretical understanding. By actively engaging in community initiatives, they play a vital role in promoting health and ensuring the safety of Liberian cities. Through awareness campaigns, practical interventions, and collaborative efforts, Environmental Volunteers become agents of positive change.

3.1.3.4 Contribution to Cleanliness and Safety

THE RIPPLE EFFECT OF CEPRES' Environmental Volunteers reaches into the very fabric of Liberian cities. Graduates actively contribute to the cleanliness of urban spaces, creating safer environments for residents. Their hands-on approach, coupled with a deep understanding of environmental issues, transforms them into key contributors to the well-being of their communities.

In conclusion, the graduation of Environmental Volunteers at CEPRES International University is not merely an academic milestone but a transformative journey towards community empowerment. By shaping individuals committed to environmental well-being, the university ensures a lasting impact on health, safety, and the overall quality of life in Liberian cities.

3.1.4 Community Engagement and Impact:

CEPRES INTERNATIONAL University stands as a beacon of academic excellence and community commitment, actively engaging with diverse communities to bring about positive change. The institution doesn't merely exist within the confines of classrooms; it extends its reach to actively impact the lives of local populations.

3.1.4.1 Initiatives in Waste Management

CEPRES TAKES A PROACTIVE stance on environmental sustainability by implementing initiatives in waste management. Through awareness programs, practical interventions, and collaboration with local authorities, the university contributes to the reduction of environmental hazards associated with improper waste disposal.

3.1.4.2 Water Testing and Treatment Initiatives

RECOGNIZING THE CRITICAL importance of clean water, CEPRES invests in initiatives related to water testing and treatment. By providing communities with access to safe and clean water sources, the institution addresses a fundamental aspect of public health. These efforts significantly contribute to preventing waterborne diseases and promoting overall well-being.

3.1.4.3 Holistic Health Promotion

THE COMMITMENT TO COMMUNITY well-being extends to health promotion initiatives. CEPRES actively involves itself in health awareness campaigns, preventive health measures, and partnerships with local healthcare providers. By addressing health concerns at the grassroots level, the institution becomes a catalyst for positive change in community health outcomes.

3.1.4.4 Beyond Imparting Knowledge

CEPRES' COMMUNITY-FOCUSED efforts go beyond the traditional role of an educational institution. While knowledge dissemination remains a core function, the active involvement in community initiatives showcases a commitment to being a catalyst for change. The institution actively contributes to the improvement of the well-being of local populations.

3.1.4.5 Creating Lasting Impact

THROUGH THESE COMMUNITY engagement initiatives, CEPRES International University creates a lasting impact on the communities it serves. The institution becomes a driving force for positive change, emphasizing the practical application of knowledge in addressing real-world challenges. By actively participating in the improvement of living conditions, CEPRES embodies the principles of community-centric education.

In conclusion, CEPRES' community engagement and impact initiatives exemplify a holistic approach to education. By actively addressing environmental, health, and societal challenges, the institution demonstrates its commitment to creating a positive and lasting impact on the communities it collaborates with.

3.1.5 Collaboration with Gbarnga City Corporation:

THE IMPACT OF CEPRES International University extends far beyond the confines of its campus, and the recognition of its graduates by the Gbarnga City Corporation stands as a testament to the practical value of CEPRES programs.

. . . .

Figure 3: Working with Gbarnga City Corporation, the AFL and local EPA Authority to clean Gbarnga, 2016

3.1.5.1 City Cleaning Collaboration with Gbarnga City Corporation

THE GBARNGA CITY CORPORATION, recognizing the skills and dedication of CEPRES graduates, has actively engaged their services for city cleaning initiatives. This collaboration is not merely a testament to the academic prowess of CEPRES alumni but also an acknowledgment of the practical impact that their education has on local communities.

3.1.5.2 Practical Application of Knowledge

CEPRES PROGRAMS ARE designed to instill practical skills and a sense of social responsibility in students. The decision by the Gbarnga City Corporation to hire CEPRES graduates for city cleaning initiatives is a clear indication that the knowledge and expertise gained at the institution translate into tangible contributions to community development.

3.1.5.3 Reinforcing CEPRES' Role in Societal Development

THIS COLLABORATION reinforces CEPRES International University's pivotal role as a contributor to societal development. By actively participating in city cleaning initiatives, CEPRES graduates not only showcase their acquired skills but also embody the institution's commitment to producing graduates who are agents of positive change in their communities.

3.1.5.4 Strategic Partnership with the Armed Forces of Liberia

IN 2017, CEPRES TOOK a significant step in community service by partnering with the Armed Forces of Liberia for city cleaning services in Gbarnga. This collaboration showcased the institution's dedication to actively participating in the improvement of the local environment and fostering partnerships with key stakeholders for the greater good.

3.1.5.5 Building a Sustainable Future

THE COLLABORATION BETWEEN CEPRES graduates and the Gbarnga City Corporation is a story of mutual benefit. Graduates find meaningful avenues to apply their skills, contributing to the cleanliness and well-being of Gbarnga City, while the city gains dedicated and skilled professionals.

The recognition of CEPRES graduates by the Gbarnga City Corporation and the strategic partnership with the Armed Forces of Liberia exemplify the practical impact of CEPRES programs on local communities. Beyond academic excellence, CEPRES International University actively contributes to societal development through the practical application of knowledge and strategic collaborations.

3.2 Graduation of Environmental Volunteers and Their Impact:

ONE OF THE DISTINCTIVE initiatives undertaken by CEPRES International University is the training of Environmental Volunteers, a program that not only reflects the institution's commitment to community engagement but also highlights its practical approach to addressing environmental and public health challenges.

3.2.1 Training Environmental Volunteers:

CEPRES INTERNATIONAL University has always understood the transformative power of hands-on experience, especially in addressing pressing environmental challenges. In alignment with this vision, the institution launched a groundbreaking program aimed at training Environmental Volunteers. This initiative reflects CEPRES' commitment to fostering a generation of graduates actively engaged in real-world problem-solving.

3.2.1.1 Purposeful Training for Positive Community Impact

THE PROGRAM GOES BEYOND traditional academic boundaries, seeking to equip individuals with both knowledge and practical skills essential for making a positive impact in their communities. By training Environmental Volunteers, CEPRES addresses the critical need for grassroots involvement in environmental issues and emphasizes the role each individual can play in creating a sustainable future.

3.2.1.2 Extension of CEPRES' Commitment to Excellence

THE ENVIRONMENTAL VOLUNTEER Training Program serves as an extension of CEPRES' overarching commitment to producing graduates who are not only academically competent but also socially responsible and actively involved in addressing real-world challenges. This holistic approach to education aligns with the institution's vision of nurturing well-rounded individuals capable of contributing meaningfully to society.

3.2.1.3 Addressing Environmental Challenges at the Local Level

RECOGNIZING THE IMPORTANCE of localized efforts in tackling global environmental challenges, CEPRES' training program focuses on empowering volunteers to address issues specific to their communities. By instilling a sense of responsibility and providing practical skills, the program aims to create a network of change agents capable of initiating positive environmental actions at the grassroots level.

3.2.1.4 Creating a Community of Environmental Stewards

THROUGH THIS INITIATIVE, CEPRES envisions the creation of a community of environmental stewards who not only understand the intricacies of environmental issues but are also equipped to implement sustainable solutions. By fostering a sense of ownership and empowerment, the program aims to inspire volunteers to become lifelong advocates for environmental conservation.

3.2.1.5 Contributing to Sustainable Development Goals

CEPRES' ENVIRONMENTAL Volunteer Training Program aligns with global efforts to achieve sustainable development goals. By empowering individuals to actively participate in environmental conservation, the program contributes to broader initiatives aimed at creating a more sustainable and resilient future for communities and the planet.

In summary, CEPRES International University's Environmental Volunteer Training Program is a testament to the institution's commitment to excellence and community engagement. By training individuals to become proactive agents of positive change, CEPRES ensures that its graduates are not just recipients of knowledge but active contributors to a better and more sustainable world.

3.2.2 Objectives of the Environmental Volunteer Training Program:

ONE OF THE PRIMARY objectives of CEPRES International University's Environmental Volunteer Training Program is to redirect the focus of young people from prevailing social issues to pressing environmental concerns. By instilling an understanding of the critical role each individual plays in environmental conservation, the program continues to inspire a generation that prioritizes the well-being of the planet.

3.2.2.1 Advocacy for the Environment:

THE PROGRAM AIMS TO go beyond basic awareness, actively training volunteers to become advocates for the environment. Through education and practical experience, participants are equipped with the knowledge and skills needed to champion environmental causes. By fostering a sense of responsibility and empowerment, CEPRES intends to create a network of individuals capable of influencing positive change in their communities.

3.2.2.2 Community Health and Cleanliness:

PARTICIPATING IN ACTIVITIES that contribute to community health and cleanliness is another key objective of the program. CEPRES recognizes the interconnectedness of environmental well-being and public health. Volunteers are trained to implement initiatives that not only enhance the cleanliness of their surroundings but also contribute to the overall health and well-being of their communities.

3.2.2.3 Raising Awareness on Climate Change:

THE ENVIRONMENTAL VOLUNTEER Training Program places a strong emphasis on raising awareness about the consequences of climate change. Volunteers are educated on the challenges posed by climate change and are empowered to promote climate resilience within their communities. By fostering a deeper understanding of environmental issues, CEPRES aims to create advocates who actively work towards sustainable solutions.

3.2.2.4 Promoting Climate Resilience:

BEYOND AWARENESS, THE program encourages volunteers to actively engage in promoting climate resilience. By imparting practical skills and knowledge, participants are prepared to take meaningful actions that contribute to building resilience in the face of changing climate patterns. This objective aligns with broader global efforts to address the impact of climate change at the community level.

In conclusion, the objectives of CEPRES' Environmental Volunteer Training Program extend beyond mere education. The program is designed to create a cadre of advocates and change agents who, through their redirected focus, advocacy efforts, community engagement, and contributions to climate resilience, play a vital role in creating a sustainable and environmentally conscious future.

3.2.3 Achievements and Success Stories:

CEPRES INTERNATIONAL University proudly celebrates the successful graduations from its Environmental Volunteer Training Program, marking the culmination of rigorous training for individuals committed to making a positive impact. The program's achievements resonate not only in the academic realm but, more significantly, in the tangible contributions its graduates have made to environmental initiatives.

3.2.3.1 Agents of Change:

THE SUCCESS STORIES of the program extend beyond the conferral of certificates. Graduates of the Environmental Volunteer program have emerged as true agents of change, actively and purposefully engaging in environmental initiatives across Liberia. These individuals, equipped with the knowledge and skills acquired during their training, have become instrumental in fostering positive transformations within their communities.

3.2.3.2 Contributions to Environmental Initiatives:

CEPRES TAKES PRIDE in the fact that its graduates are not passive beneficiaries of education but dynamic contributors to environmental causes. Whether it's spearheading local cleanup campaigns, promoting sustainable practices, or advocating for environmental awareness, these individuals are making significant strides in addressing ecological challenges. Their contributions stand as testament to the practical impact of the Environmental Volunteer Training Program.

3.2.3.3 Creating a Ripple Effect:

THE ACHIEVEMENTS OF the program go beyond individual success stories; they create a ripple effect within communities. As graduates actively participate in environmental initiatives, they inspire others to join the cause. This multiplier effect amplifies the program's impact, fostering a broader community-driven approach to environmental stewardship.

3.2.3.4 Building a Network of Environmental Champions:

CEPRES SEES THE ACHIEVEMENTS of its Environmental Volunteer Training Program as the foundation for building a network of environmental champions. These individuals, connected by their shared commitment to positive change, form a community of practice dedicated to addressing environmental challenges in Liberia. The program's success stories serve as beacons, guiding others toward a path of active engagement and meaningful contribution.

In summary, the achievements and success stories of CEPRES' Environmental Volunteer Program showcase not only the effectiveness of the training but also the transformative potential of education when applied with purpose and dedication. The program stands as a beacon of inspiration, illuminating the path toward a more sustainable and environmentally conscious future in Liberia.

3.2.4 Community Engagement and Impact:

CEPRES INTERNATIONAL University takes pride in the transformative journey of its graduates, now Environmental Volunteers, who have transitioned from academic excellence to active community engagement. Armed with the knowledge and skills acquired during their training, these volunteers are making a meaningful impact on the ground, embodying the institution's commitment to practical education.

3.2.4.1 Addressing Critical Issues:

THE ENVIRONMENTAL VOLUNTEERS from CEPRES have become frontline contributors to community well-being through their active involvement in critical areas such as waste management, water testing and treatment, and health promotion. By putting their education into practice, they contribute to the resolution of real-world challenges faced by communities in Liberia.

3.2.4.2 Waste Management Prowess:

ONE OF THE STANDOUT areas of community engagement is in waste management. CEPRES graduates, now Environmental Volunteers, actively participate in waste management initiatives, contributing to the cleanliness and environmental health of their communities. Their hands-on involvement reflects a commitment to sustainable practices and a desire to create cleaner and healthier living environments.

3.2.4.3 Ensuring Clean Water Access:

WATER TESTING AND TREATMENT are vital components of the volunteers' engagement. Applying their knowledge in these areas, they work toward ensuring access to clean and safe water for local populations. By addressing water quality issues, CEPRES Environmental Volunteers play a crucial role in promoting public health and preventing waterborne diseases.

3.2.4.4 Advocates for Health Promotion:

BEYOND WASTE MANAGEMENT and water quality, the volunteers actively engage in health promotion initiatives. They serve as advocates for healthy living practices, sharing insights on preventive healthcare, and fostering awareness about the consequences of unhealthy habits. This multifaceted approach contributes to the overall well-being of communities.

3.2.4.5 Practical Applications of Education:

THE COMMUNITY ENGAGEMENT and impact created by CEPRES Environmental Volunteers exemplify the practical applications of education. By translating theoretical knowledge into actionable steps, these volunteers serve as role models, inspiring others to actively contribute to community development. Their initiatives align with CEPRES' vision of producing graduates who are not only academically proficient but also socially responsible.

In conclusion, the community engagement and impact achieved by CEPRES Environmental Volunteers underscore the institution's commitment to nurturing individuals who actively contribute to societal well-being. Through their practical initiatives, these volunteers bring positive change to communities, demonstrating the powerful intersection of education and community service.

The graduation of Environmental Volunteers not only represents an academic achievement for the individuals involved but also signifies CEPRES' success in creating a cadre of professionals actively contributing to environmental sustainability and community well-being. This initiative aligns with the institution's broader mission of stimulating public health quality and promoting environmental sanity through practical, hands-on approaches.

4 Vision and Mission of CEPRES International University

4.1 Vision for Excellence in Environmental and Public Health Education:

CEPRES INTERNATIONAL University's vision for excellence in environmental and public health education encapsulates its overarching aspirations, guiding principles, and commitment to fostering a transformative learning experience. This vision, crafted under the leadership of Dr. Mogana S. Flomo, Jr., underscores the institution's dedication to becoming a pioneering force in shaping the future of environmental and public health professionals.

4.1.1 Pinnacle of Academic Distinction:

- The vision positions CEPRES as a premier institution, aspiring to achieve the pinnacle of academic distinction in the fields of environmental and public health.
- This commitment to excellence reflects in the rigorous academic programs, faculty expertise, and the institution's overarching goal to produce highly competent graduates.

4.1.2 Interdisciplinary Instruction at all Levels:

- CEPRES envisions itself as an institution that provides interdisciplinary instruction at various levels, including certificates, diplomas, and degrees.
- This approach aims to equip students with a holistic understanding of the complex interplay between environmental factors and public health, preparing them for multifaceted roles in their professional journeys.

4.1.3 Local and International Educational Leadership:

- The vision extends beyond national borders, positioning CEPRES as a foremost international educational institution.
- By aspiring to lead not only in Liberia but also in the broader African sub-region and beyond, CEPRES sets itself apart as a global player in environmental and public health education.

4.1.4 Stimulating Public Health Quality:

- At the core of CEPRES' vision is the stimulation of public health quality in Liberia, Sub-Saharan Africa, and the world.
- The institution sees itself as a catalyst for positive change, actively contributing to the improvement of public health systems and advocating for environmental sanity through research, training, service improvement, consultancy, and advocacy.

4.1.5 Production of Competent and Self-Reliant Graduates:

- CEPRES envisions a future where its graduates emerge not only as highly competent professionals but also as self-reliant individuals.
- The institution aims to instill in its students the skills, knowledge, and ethical principles necessary for success in their chosen fields and beyond.

4.1.6 Global Educational Standards and Best Practices:

- The commitment to maintaining global educational standards and abiding by international best practices underscores CEPRES' dedication to providing a world-class education.

- This vision positions the institution as a beacon of quality, attracting students and faculty who seek a high standard of academic and professional development.

AS CEPRES INTERNATIONAL University strives toward its vision for excellence, it charts a course that transcends conventional educational paradigms. The vision articulates a bold and ambitious future for the institution, one where environmental and public health education becomes a catalyst for positive societal transformation on both local and global scales.

4.2 Mission: Stimulating Public Health Quality through Research, Training, and Service Improvement:

CEPRES INTERNATIONAL University's mission is a guiding declaration that articulates the institution's purpose, values, and the specific avenues through which it seeks to make a positive impact. The mission, crafted under the leadership of Dr. Mogana S. Flomo, Jr., embodies a commitment to excellence in public health and environmental education while actively contributing to the betterment of public health systems. Let's delve into the core components of this mission:

4.2.1 Stimulating Public Health Quality:

- At the heart of CEPRES' mission is the commitment to stimulate public health quality. This involves actively engaging in activities and initiatives that enhance the effectiveness and efficiency of public health systems.
- The term "stimulating" implies a dynamic and proactive approach, emphasizing the institution's role as a catalyst for positive change in public health.

4.2.2 Through Research, Training, and Service Improvement:

- CEPRES identifies three key pillars through which it aims to fulfill its mission: research, training, and service improvement.
- *Research:* CEPRES recognizes the importance of advancing knowledge in the fields of environmental and public health. Through rigorous research endeavors, the institution contributes to the body of academic and practical knowledge, informing evidence-based practices.
- *Training:* The mission underscores the pivotal role of education in driving positive change. CEPRES is dedicated to training the next generation of professionals in environmental and public health, ensuring they possess the skills and knowledge needed to address contemporary challenges.
- **Service Improvement:** Beyond academia, CEPRES is committed to actively improving services related to public health. This involves practical interventions and initiatives aimed at enhancing the delivery of healthcare services, particularly in the context of environmental and public health concerns.

4.2.3 Consultancy and Advocacy:

- The mission extends to consultancy and advocacy, recognizing the importance of leveraging expertise to influence policies and practices.
- *Consultancy:* CEPRES positions itself as a resource for expertise, offering consultancy services to organizations and entities seeking guidance in matters related to environmental and health sciences.
- *Advocacy:* The institution advocates for policies and practices

that promote public health and environmental sustainability. This advocacy role aligns with CEPRES' commitment to being an active participant in shaping the broader landscape of public health.

4.2.4 Premier Standard of Tertiary Education:

- CEPRES' mission includes a commitment to providing a premier standard of tertiary education.
- This involves not only the delivery of high-quality academic programs but also a holistic approach to education that nurtures the development of well-rounded and ethically conscious individuals.

4.2.5 Global Educational Standards and Best Practices:

- In line with the mission, CEPRES is dedicated to maintaining global educational standards and adhering to international best practices.
- This commitment ensures that graduates of CEPRES receive an education that is recognized and respected on a global scale, enhancing their opportunities for success in diverse professional settings.

CEPRES INTERNATIONAL University's mission articulates a holistic approach to its role in society, encompassing education, research, service improvement, consultancy, and advocacy. This multifaceted mission positions the institution as a dynamic force for positive change, actively contributing to the enhancement of public health quality and environmental sustainability.

4.3 Goals and Objectives for Providing Premier Tertiary Education:

CEPRES INTERNATIONAL University's commitment to providing premier tertiary education is accompanied by specific goals and objectives that outline the institution's strategic roadmap. Crafted under the leadership of Dr. Mogana S. Flomo, Jr., these goals reflect CEPRES' dedication to excellence, accessibility, and global relevance in tertiary education. Let's explore these goals and objectives in detail:

4.3.1 Providing Premier Tertiary Education:

CEPRES INTERNATIONAL University is driven by a bold vision to be a distinguished institution, celebrated for offering premier tertiary education in the specialized domains of environmental and public health. This aspiration is not merely a goal but a commitment to delivering educational experiences that stand out on the global stage.

4.3.1.1 Strategic Objectives:

TO REALIZE THIS VISION, CEPRES has outlined strategic objectives that serve as guiding principles in its pursuit of premier tertiary education:

High-Quality Academic Programs:
CEPRES is dedicated to implementing academic programs of the highest quality, benchmarked against global standards. These programs are designed to provide students with a comprehensive and cutting-edge education that prepares them for the challenges and opportunities in their respective fields.

Learning Environment Excellence:
The institution fosters an environment that goes beyond conventional learning. CEPRES aims to create a space conducive to advanced learning, critical thinking, and the practical application of

knowledge. This approach ensures that students not only grasp theoretical concepts but also develop the skills needed for real-world scenarios.

Expert Faculty:

At the heart of premier education is a faculty comprised of experienced and highly qualified professionals. CEPRES is committed to assembling a team of educators who are not only experts in their respective fields but are also passionate about academic excellence. The faculty serves as mentors, guiding students on their academic journeys.

Curricular Innovation:

Recognizing the dynamic nature of knowledge and the evolving landscape of environmental and public health, CEPRES places a premium on continuously updating curricula. This involves incorporating emerging trends, leveraging new technologies, and integrating the latest research findings. The institution is committed to ensuring that its programs remain relevant and forward-looking.

4.3.1.2 The Blueprint for Excellence:

CEPRES INTERNATIONAL University's commitment to providing premier tertiary education is more than a statement; it is a blueprint for excellence. By aligning its goals with global standards, creating an enriching learning environment, nurturing a faculty of distinction, and embracing curricular innovation, CEPRES is laying the foundation for a new era of educational distinction. Through this commitment, the institution is poised to shape the future of environmental and public health education, producing graduates who stand as beacons of knowledge and impact.

4.3.2 Producing Competent Graduates:

GOAL:

CEPRES International University is on a mission to shape graduates into well-rounded individuals who transcend mere academic proficiency. The goal is to produce professionals equipped not only with theoretical knowledge but also with practical skills and a strong ethical foundation essential for success in the complex realms of environmental and public health.

4.3.2.1 Objectives:

COMPREHENSIVE AND INTERDISCIPLINARY Education:
CEPRES recognizes that excellence goes beyond subject mastery. The institution is committed to offering comprehensive and interdisciplinary programs. These programs are meticulously crafted to provide students with a holistic understanding of environmental and public health, integrating various facets to create a more profound educational experience.

Practical Integration:
The university understands the significance of practical skills in real-world scenarios. To achieve this, CEPRES has set objectives to integrate practical components, internships, and hands-on experiences directly into the curriculum. This ensures that graduates are not only knowledgeable in theory but are also adept at applying their knowledge in practical settings.

Cultivating a Learning Environment:
Beyond academic prowess, CEPRES is committed to fostering a learning environment that cultivates ethical behavior, critical thinking, and effective communication. These qualities are considered essential for graduates to navigate the complexities of their professions with integrity and to engage in meaningful dialogue within their respective fields.

4.3.2.2 The Ethical and Practical Advantage:

CEPRES INTERNATIONAL University's vision extends beyond conventional education. By marrying theoretical knowledge with practical skills and ethical principles, the institution aims to provide its graduates with a distinct advantage. The focus on interdisciplinary education, practical integration, and the cultivation of a robust learning environment positions CEPRES graduates as ethical leaders and practitioners capable of making meaningful contributions to the fields of environmental and public health. The goal is not just academic success but the development of professionals who can drive positive change in society.

4.3.3 Multipurpose Environmental and Health Professionals:

4.3.3.1 Goal:

CEPRES INTERNATIONAL University is dedicated to producing graduates who embody versatility, capable of tackling an array of challenges in the expansive fields of environmental and public health. The goal is to nurture professionals with diverse skills, ensuring they can navigate multifaceted issues in these critical sectors.

4.3.3.2 Objectives:

SPECIALIZED TRAINING:
CEPRES recognizes the need for specialization in addressing the intricate challenges of environmental and public health. To fulfill this objective, the university provides specialized training in areas such as environmental monitoring, waste management, community health,

agriculture, education, and more. This ensures that graduates possess in-depth knowledge and expertise in their chosen domains.

Adaptability in Diverse Settings:

The curriculum at CEPRES is designed with a focus on equipping students with versatile skills that make them adaptable to diverse professional settings. The intention is to mold graduates who can seamlessly transition between different roles and effectively contribute to various facets of environmental and public health.

Community Engagement and Social Responsibility:

CEPRES places great importance on community engagement and social responsibility. Graduates are instilled with an understanding of the broader impact of their work. Emphasizing the significance of giving back to communities, the university aims to produce professionals who not only excel in their individual capacities but also actively contribute to societal well-being.

4.3.3.3 Versatility in Action:

CEPRES INTERNATIONAL University's vision goes beyond traditional education. By focusing on specialized training, adaptability, and a strong sense of social responsibility, the institution envisions its graduates as multipurpose environmental and health professionals. These professionals are not confined by narrow expertise but possess a broad skill set, making them invaluable contributors to the dynamic and evolving landscape of environmental and public health.

4.3.4 Affordable Foreign-Accredited Certificates, Diplomas, and Degrees:

4.3.4.1 Goal:

CEPRES INTERNATIONAL University is committed to breaking barriers to quality education by providing affordable foreign-accredited certificates, diplomas, and degrees. The goal is to make high-quality education accessible to a broader range of students, ensuring that financial constraints or geographical distances do not hinder educational pursuits.

4.3.4.2 Objectives:

ESTABLISHING INTERNATIONAL Accreditation Partnerships:
CEPRES acknowledges the importance of international accreditation in ensuring the quality and recognition of its educational programs. The institution actively seeks partnerships with reputable international educational institutions to secure accreditation. This not only enhances the credibility of CEPRES but also opens doors for its students globally.

Financial Aid and Scholarship Programs:
To enhance accessibility, CEPRES implements robust financial aid and scholarship programs. By doing so, the university aims to alleviate financial barriers that might hinder students from pursuing higher education. These programs create opportunities for talented individuals who might otherwise face challenges in funding their education.

Hybrid Learning Models:
Recognizing the diverse needs and geographical locations of students, CEPRES facilitates both classroom and distance learning education. This approach ensures that individuals from various

backgrounds can access quality education without being constrained by their physical location. The adoption of hybrid learning models aligns with the university's commitment to inclusivity.

4.3.4.3 Empowering Through Accessible Education:

CEPRES INTERNATIONAL University's vision goes beyond the confines of traditional educational models. By establishing international accreditation, offering financial aid and scholarships, and embracing hybrid learning, the institution strives to empower individuals worldwide. The goal is to create a learning environment where accessibility is not a barrier, enabling students to embark on educational journeys that lead to personal and professional growth.

4.3.5 Positive Influence on Higher Institutions of Learning in Liberia:

4.3.5.1 Goal:

CEPRES INTERNATIONAL University aspires to be a positive force, influencing the professional and ethical standards of higher institutions of learning in Liberia. The goal is to contribute to the overall enhancement of Liberia's educational landscape.

4.3.5.2 Objectives:

COLLABORATIVE BEST Practices:
CEPRES recognizes the power of collaboration in fostering positive change. The institution actively collaborates with other higher education institutions, sharing best practices and collectively working towards the improvement of educational standards in Liberia. Through

these collaborations, CEPRES aims to create a network that uplifts the entire educational ecosystem.

Modeling Ethical and Professional Standards:

CEPRES commits to serving as a model for ethical and professional standards in both academic and administrative practices. By adhering to the highest standards of integrity, transparency, and professionalism, the university aims to set an example for other institutions. This involves cultivating an environment where ethical conduct is not just encouraged but ingrained in the institutional culture.

Contributing to Educational Policies:

CEPRES actively contributes to the development of educational policies that promote excellence and inclusivity. By participating in policy discussions and initiatives, the institution seeks to shape a regulatory framework that supports academic integrity, quality education, and equal opportunities for all students.

4.3.5.3 Driving Positive Change:

CEPRES INTERNATIONAL University sees itself as a catalyst for positive change in Liberia's higher education landscape. Through collaboration, ethical modeling, and policy contributions, the institution aims to create a ripple effect that uplifts the standards of education across the country. By actively engaging with other institutions and advocating for policies that foster excellence, CEPRES strives to be a driving force in the continuous improvement of Liberia's higher education sector.

4.3.6 Global Educational Standards and Best Practices:

4.3.6.1 Goal:

CEPRES INTERNATIONAL University is dedicated to maintaining global educational standards and adhering to international best practices. The goal is to ensure that the institution's programs and graduates meet or exceed international expectations, enhancing their competitiveness on a global scale.

4.3.6.2 Objectives:

REGULAR PROGRAM REVIEW and Benchmarking:
CEPRES commits to regularly reviewing and benchmarking its academic programs against global standards. By staying informed about the latest developments and benchmarks in international education, the institution ensures that its curriculum remains relevant, up-to-date, and aligned with the best practices observed worldwide.

Engagement in International Collaborations:
To stay abreast of global trends and practices, CEPRES actively engages in international collaborations, partnerships, and exchanges. These initiatives provide faculty and students with exposure to diverse educational approaches, methodologies, and perspectives. By fostering international relationships, the university enriches its educational environment and contributes to the global exchange of knowledge.

Ensuring Competitive Graduates:
CEPRES places a strong emphasis on preparing graduates who are not only competitive locally but also on a global scale. The institution ensures that its academic programs equip students with the skills, knowledge, and mindset needed to succeed in an international context. This includes incorporating elements that cultivate global awareness, cross-cultural understanding, and adaptability.

4.3.6.3 Global Educational Excellence:

CEPRES INTERNATIONAL University's commitment to global educational excellence is woven into its fabric. Through continuous review, international engagements, and a focus on producing globally competitive graduates, the institution positions itself as a hub for educational quality that extends beyond national boundaries. By adhering to global standards and embracing best practices, CEPRES prepares its students to thrive in a diverse and interconnected world.

As CEPRES International University pursues its goals and objectives, the institution envisions a future where its graduates not only excel in their chosen fields but also contribute meaningfully to societal well-being and environmental sustainability.

5 Recognition, Partnerships and Scholarships

5.1 The International Academic and Management Association (IAMA)

Figure 4:(*IAMA – IAMA*, n.d.) THE INTERNATIONAL ACADEMIC and Management Association (IAMA) is a notable private, not-for-profit association dedicated to promoting education as a fundamental right for everyone. Dr. Mogana S. Flomo, Jr. serves as a member of the Board of Trustees for IAMA. Established in 2013 and registered under the Indian Trust Act, IAMA has rapidly grown to become one of the fastest-growing associations globally.

Key tenets of IAMA's educational philosophy include providing qualitative, affordable, dynamic, flexible, inclusive, borderless, and industry-centric education. The association serves over 200 educational institutions, government agencies, and government-backed entities across 44 countries, impacting thousands of students annually through internationalization efforts.

In 2022, IAMA achieved significant milestones, including:

1. Becoming an official partner of the World Health Organization (WHO) through the PMNCH initiative, focusing on the health of women, children, and adolescents.

"

2. Attaining designation as a UN Partner organization (NGO) for projects related to UNICEF, WFP, UNHCR, and UNFPA.
3. Receiving full accreditation from QAHE (Quality Assurance in Higher Education) as an organization of high standing.
4. Obtaining full accreditation from EEQA (European Quality Assurance Register for Higher Education).

IAMA has expanded its scope to address healthcare, waste management, and renewable energy. To support these initiatives, a subsidiary named IAMA International Tradelinks Pvt. Ltd. (IITPL) was created. The healthcare project involves establishing collaborative medical colleges in developing nations, upgrading existing hospitals, and providing access to affordable generic medicines.

In the area of waste management, IAMA plans to introduce technology to convert waste into domestic bio-fuel and organic fertilizer. IITPL also aims to promote the usage of solar energy in collaboration with governments and private players to address electric power challenges in these countries.

Furthermore, IAMA successfully launched its university, the IAMA International Open University of Florida, registered in Florida, USA, in 2022. Additionally, the School of Vocational and Technical Education (IAMA – SVTE) was inaugurated to promote employability and entrepreneurship trades and skills.

The comprehensive approach of IAMA, spanning education, healthcare, waste management, and renewable energy, reflects its commitment to making a positive impact globally.

5.1.1 Status of CEPRES International University in the IAMA

CEPRES INTERNATIONAL University's affiliation with the International Academic and Management Association (IAMA) began in 2015. Over the years, the university has demonstrated a commitment to the principles and values of IAMA. As a recognition of its sustained engagement and contributions, CEPRES International University has achieved the esteemed status of Lifetime Membership in IAMA, starting from the year 2022.

Figure 5: President of IAMA Presents Lifetime Membership certificate to CIU

This achievement signifies the university's dedication to promoting education as a fundamental right and its active participation in the initiatives and programs facilitated by IAMA. Lifetime Membership is a significant acknowledgment of CEPRES International University's ongoing commitment to the goals and mission of the association.

5.1.2 The IAMA Center of Excellence

IN 2015, A SIGNIFICANT milestone was achieved at CEPRES International University with the establishment of the International Academic and Management Association Center of Excellence (IAMA-CoE). This center, rooted in the educational vision of IAMA, was created to deliver high-quality, internationally recognized certificates, diplomas, and degrees at various academic levels, including Associate, Bachelor, and Masters.

The IAMA-CoE at CEPRES International quickly became a hub for academic excellence, embodying the commitment to provide learners with education that meets global standards. The center's curriculum and programs reflect the prestigious standards set forth by the International Academic and Management Association.

In 2017, the inaugural cohort of students from the IAMA-CoE celebrated a momentous occasion as they graduated with a range of academic achievements, including certificates, Associate degrees, and Postgraduate Diplomas. This marked the first batch of successful graduates from the IAMA programs at CEPRES International University.

As one of the oldest international institutions hosted by CEPRES International University, the IAMA-CoE has played a pivotal role in shaping the academic landscape of the university. It continues to uphold the principles of quality education and international recognition, contributing to the global vision of both CEPRES International University and the International Academic and Management Association.

5.2 Accreditation

IN 2016, CEPRES INTERNATIONAL University achieved Provisional Accreditation from the National Commission on High Education (NCHE), marking a significant milestone in its commitment to maintaining high educational standards. This provisional accreditation, initially valid for two years, demonstrated the university's dedication to meeting the rigorous criteria set by the NCHE.

Building on this achievement, in 2018, CEPRES International University further solidified its standing by attaining Full Accreditation from the NCHE. This recognition, valid for an additional two years, reflected the university's continuous efforts to enhance its educational offerings and infrastructure.

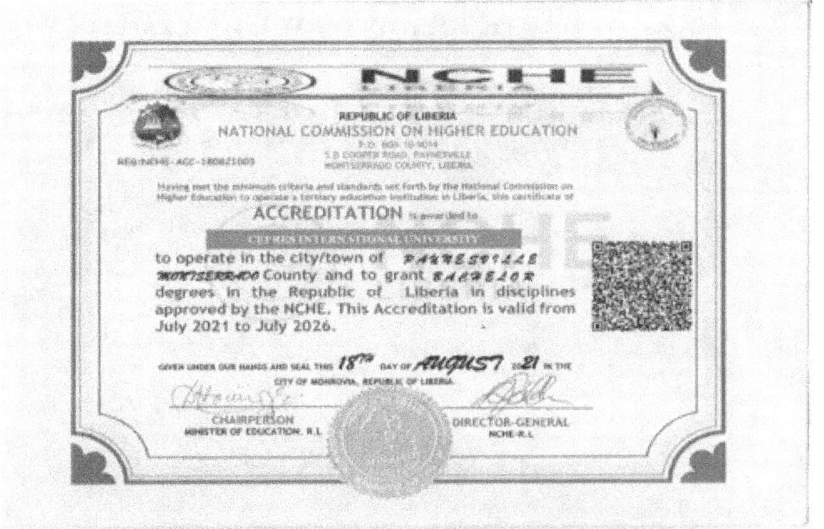

Figure 6: NCHE Accreditation Certificate to CEPRES International University, 2021 - 2026

The year 2021 marked a pivotal moment for the university as it secured Full Accreditation from the NCHE once again. This accreditation, now extended for a substantial five-year period, is a testament to the institution's sustained commitment to academic excellence and compliance with established standards. The accompanying certificate, with the identification number NCHE-ACC-180821003, signifies the university's recognition by the national education regulatory body and its approval to continue providing quality education for the specified duration.

5.3 Texila American University

Figure 7:("About-Our-Accredited-Online-University-Texila-American-University," n.d.)

IN 2015, CEPRES INTERNATIONAL University (CIU) forged a significant partnership with Texila American University (TAU) in Guyana. This collaboration led to the establishment of a Learning Management Center (LMC) of Texila American University at CIU. The LMC plays a crucial role in the recruitment and verification of academic credentials for applicants, registering students at TAU through a secure portal, and facilitating further processing by the central registry of TAU. Several students from Liberia have benefited from this collaboration, gaining access to world-class education.

Texila American University, known for its tradition of innovation and research, has been a key player in developing minds in the field of medicine for over a decade. The university is committed to pushing the boundaries of knowledge, making a positive impact on students' lives, and achieving recognition on the international stage.

5.3.1 Texila Vision and Mission:

VISION: To be recognized as a leader committed to excellence in higher education, research, and innovation that meets the aspirations of the global community.

Mission: To redefine and revolutionize international education by offering updated, modern, and excellent training in various areas. Additionally, the mission includes observing high standards of ethics, integrity, compassionate care for students and the community, and making TAU proud of being the most sustainable university globally.

5.3.2 Texila Values & Culture:

EXCELLENCE IS ACHIEVED by captivating the integral value system, focusing on customers, people, leadership, integrity, innovation and creativity, responsibility, and global growth.

The partnership between CEPRES International University and Texila American University underscores a commitment to providing quality education and opportunities for students in Liberia and beyond.

5.4 Sharda University and Hospital

Figure 8:(*Sharda University - A Truly Global University*, n.d.)

IN 2022, CEPRES INTERNATIONAL University (CIU) marked a significant partnership by signing an agreement with Sharda University and Sharda Hospital. This collaboration is multifaceted, encompassing educational opportunities for students as well as avenues for advanced medical treatment.

As part of this collaboration, CIU, serving as the original partners and legal representative, is entrusted with the recruitment of students aspiring to pursue Bachelor's, Master's, or Ph.D. degrees in India. This initiative reflects the commitment to providing educational opportunities that transcend geographical boundaries.

Sharda University, the esteemed partner in this collaboration, is characterized not only as an educational institution but as a diverse community that values cultural inclusivity and respects differences in religion, age, gender, and socio-economic status. The university is dedicated to constantly upgrading its academic offerings and services to meet the evolving demands of the global workforce.

Reasons highlighted for choosing India as an educational destination include its status as the fastest-growing economy, the second-largest pool of engineers and scientists, and the affordability of education and cost of living. India's cultural richness, diverse locations, and being the world's second-largest English-speaking country further contribute to its appeal.

Sharda University, specifically chosen for its commitment to providing multidisciplinary education, boasts several accolades and recognitions, including being the No. 1 university in India with the highest number of international students. The degrees offered by Sharda University are internationally recognized and approved by the UGC (University Grants Commission), Government of India.

Additional features of Sharda University include a 900+ bedded super-speciality hospital on campus, various on-campus residence facilities, and over 250 functional Memoranda of Understanding (MOUs) tie-ups for semester exchange and free tuition fee programs. These collaborations provide global exposure and limitless opportunities for students at Sharda University.

This partnership between CEPRES International University and Sharda University signifies a commitment to global education and healthcare, facilitating a bridge for students in Liberia to access quality education and advanced medical treatments in India.

5.5 Institute of Real Estate and Finance

IN 2022, CEPRES INTERNATIONAL University (CIU) forged a significant partnership with IREF Global Learning Pvt Ltd, an educational institution based in Pune, India. The collaboration aimed to bring quality education in real estate, construction, and finance to students in Liberia.

Figure 9:(*Top* Real Estate and Construction Management Institute in India | 1000+ Alumni's, n.d.)

The Memorandum of Understanding (MoU) outlined key aspects of the partnership. CIU, as an authorized associate partner, played a pivotal role in marketing and facilitating admissions for IREF's programs. In return, IREF granted CIU the right to operate under the name "IREF Executive Education and Business Centre" in Liberia.

The partnership involved mutual responsibilities. CIU was responsible for guiding and supporting the agreed-upon programs, assisting in student enrollment, and allowing IREF to use its logo for promotional purposes. IREF, in turn, committed to ensuring program completion, providing job assistance, and sharing incentives with CIU.

Financial arrangements were outlined, including a lump sum and association fees. The partnership also allowed CIU to collect fees from students, with revenue sharing arrangements through online payment gateways or bank deposits.

The collaboration extended beyond existing programs, with provisions for introducing new courses based on mutual understanding. The emphasis on a Learning Management System (LMS) facilitated online education, connecting students across geographical boundaries.

The partnership aimed for a holistic approach, incorporating scholarship programs, periodic reviews, and a commitment to adapt to market needs. The MoU specified the termination conditions and outlined a dispute resolution mechanism.

In essence, the partnership between CIU and IREF was a strategic alliance to extend educational opportunities, leveraging the strengths of both institutions. It sought to provide a diverse range of programs, foster global connections through online education, and contribute to the educational growth of Liberia.

5.6 Lincoln University College

Figure 10:(*Lincoln University College | Top Private University Degree & Medical College In Malaysia*, n.d.)

THIS MEMORANDUM OF Understanding (MoU) was established on July 30, 2021, among CEPRES International University (First Party) in Liberia, Lincoln University College (Second Party) in

Malaysia, and the International Academic and Management Association (Third Party) based in India. The purpose of this collaboration was to facilitate the implementation of Post Graduate and Doctoral Programs in Medicine and Allied Health Sciences at CIU's facility, with the involvement of LUC's expertise and IAMA's representation.

5.6.1 Roles and Responsibilities:

FIRST PARTY (CIU):

- Provide necessary infrastructure for classes and clinical training.
- Arrange hostels/dormitories for students.
- Obtain necessary permissions and approvals from Liberian authorities.
- Indemnify the Second and Third Parties from any acts during program delivery.
- Handle marketing, admissions, and fee collection.
- Ensure remuneration and expenses for teaching and support staff.
- Take responsibility for travel expenses related to the collaboration.

Second Party (LUC):

- Develop/provide curriculum for agreed programs.
- Issue degrees to graduating students.
- Identify/shortlist teaching doctors.
- Monitor and audit academic delivery.
- Evaluate students in theory and clinical training.
- Appoint a Single Point of Contact (SPOC) for the collaboration.

- Determine fees for agreed programs in consultation with other parties.

Third Party (IAMA):

- Act as an intermediary in the collaboration.
- Identify resources for agreed programs.
- Assist in procuring necessary resources.
- Help in identifying teaching resources.
- Assist in the Academic Audit Process.
- Conduct an audit of the Evaluation Process.

5.6.2 Programs & Fees:

THE SPECIFIC POST GRADUATE and Doctoral Degree programs, along with the corresponding fees, were to be decided and added to the MoU as Annexure I.

Revenue Distribution: The distribution of revenue among the First, Second, and Third Parties was to be mutually decided and added to the MoU as Annexure II.

5.6.3 Validity and Termination:

THE MOU WAS INITIALLY valid for six years, with the possibility of renewal on mutual consent. Either party could terminate the collaboration by providing a one-year advance notice. In case of termination, the parties committed to prioritizing the interests of students, ensuring minimal adverse impact, and taking care of the enrolled students until the termination date.

5.7 Scholarships

CEPRES INTERNATIONAL University is committed to fostering accessible and quality education by offering various scholarships, each addressing specific needs within the community. These scholarships, initiated by the university's Founder, aim to empower deserving students who might not have financial means to pursue their educational aspirations. Unlike traditional scholarship programs funded by external sources, these scholarships are exclusively sponsored by the university to identify and address diverse educational needs. Here are some of the scholarships provided by CIU:

5.7.1 International Academic and Management Association Scholarship:

INTRODUCED IN 2017, this scholarship is dedicated to providing educational opportunities for deserving students across Liberia. Beneficiaries are selected from diverse communities, reflecting the university's commitment to inclusivity. The scholarship is named in recognition of the strong educational partnership between CIU and the International Academic and Management Association (IAMA).

5.7.2 Dr. Mogana S. Flomo, Jr. Scholarship:

THIS SCHOLARSHIP FOCUSES on supporting individuals with special needs and contributes to the development of agriculture in Liberia. It enables beneficiaries to pursue education in sustainable agriculture, aligning with the goal of promoting food security in the country. Many students have successfully accessed quality education through this scholarship.

5.7.3 Security Sector Development Education Scholarship:

LAUNCHED ON FEBRUARY 10, 2018, this scholarship targets members of the Armed Forces of Liberia, the Liberia National Police, the Liberia Immigration Service (LIS), Liberia Fire Service (LFS), and the Drugs Enforcement Agency (DEA). Envisioned by Dr. Mogana S.

Flomo, Jr., the scholarship aims to enhance the education and training of security sector personnel in critical areas such as disaster management, environmental science, and related fields. Numerous Liberian security officers are currently benefiting from this initiative.

5.7.4 Special In-Service Teachers Scholarship:

THIS SCHOLARSHIP OFFERS a flexible pathway for unqualified or semi-qualified teachers to upgrade their teaching skills and earn degrees in various educational disciplines. The program, designed for weekend classes, accommodates teachers working in rural areas, allowing them to attend classes without disrupting their teaching schedules. Subjects covered include Education Management, Secondary Education (Arts and Science Paths), Early Childhood Education, Primary Education, STEM Education, Teaching, and more.

5.7.5 Border Region Scholarship:

GEARED TOWARDS INDIVIDUALS working in remote areas far from universities, this scholarship provides an opportunity for online education. Courses are taught by the same experienced lecturers who teach on-campus, ensuring a consistent and high-quality learning experience. Beneficiaries can continue working in challenging areas while pursuing their education.

Through these scholarships, CEPRES International University strives to make education accessible to diverse groups, addressing specific needs within the community and contributing to the overall development of Liberia.

6.1 Study Skills and Time Management:

STUDY SKILLS AND TIME management are foundational aspects of academic success, and CEPRES International University recognizes their critical importance in preparing students for a rigorous educational journey. Dr. Mogana S. Flomo, Jr., the visionary founder of CEPRES, emphasizes the significance of these skills in the pursuit of excellence. Let's delve into the discussion of study skills and time management within the context of CEPRES International University:

6.1.1 Effective Study Techniques:

IN THE PURSUIT OF ACADEMIC success, students often face the challenge of mastering effective study techniques. CEPRES International University recognizes the multifaceted nature of learning and places a strong emphasis on equipping students with strategies that go beyond rote memorization. The university acknowledges that understanding, critical thinking, and practical application are integral components of successful learning experiences.

6.1.1.1 Active Reading Strategies

ONE CRUCIAL STUDY TECHNIQUE emphasized at CEPRES is active reading. The university advocates for techniques such as highlighting important passages, annotating texts, and engaging in reflective reading. The goal is to encourage students to interact with the material actively, promoting a deeper understanding of concepts (Smith, 2018).

6.1.1.2 Note-Taking as a Learning Aid

NOTE-TAKING IS ANOTHER fundamental aspect of effective studying. CEPRES recommends methods such as the Cornell method or the mapping approach to help students organize information systematically. By summarizing key points and connecting ideas, students enhance their retention and comprehension (Jones & Johnson, 2019).

Cornell Method

Figure 11: Cornell method of not taking

6.1.1.3 Utilizing Concept Mapping

THE USE OF CONCEPT maps is endorsed at CEPRES as a visual aid to understand the relationships between different ideas. Research indicates that concept mapping enhances meaningful learning and improves long-term retention (Novak & Cañas, 2008).

6.1.1.4 Problem-Solving Strategies

CEPRES ENCOURAGES THE application of problem-solving strategies in the learning process. Integrating problem-based learning approaches into study sessions enhances critical thinking skills and the ability to apply theoretical knowledge in practical scenarios (Savin-Baden & Major, 2004).

In summary, CEPRES International University adopts a holistic approach to study techniques, emphasizing active reading, note-taking, concept mapping, and problem-solving strategies. By incorporating these methods into their study routines, students can foster a deeper understanding of course materials, promoting academic success.

6.1.2 Time Management Strategies:

6.1.2.1 Time Management Strategies for Academic Success

EFFECTIVE TIME MANAGEMENT is crucial for academic success, helping students balance their academic responsibilities with other aspects of life. Here are key strategies to enhance time management skills:

Prioritization:

- Explanation: Identify and prioritize tasks based on their urgency and importance. Focus on high-priority assignments and activities to ensure deadlines are met.

Set SMART Goals:

- Explanation: Establish Specific, Measurable, Achievable, Relevant, and Time-bound (SMART) goals. This framework provides clarity and structure for goal-setting.

Create a Schedule:

- Explanation: Develop a daily or weekly schedule that includes dedicated time for classes, study sessions, and leisure. Stick to the schedule to create a routine.

Use Time Blocks:

- Explanation: Group similar tasks together in time blocks. This minimizes context switching and helps maintain focus on specific types of activities during designated periods.

Utilize a Planner or Apps:

- Explanation: Use planners or digital apps to organize tasks, deadlines, and appointments. Set reminders to stay on track and avoid forgetting important commitments.

Break Tasks into Manageable Steps:

- Explanation: Divide larger tasks into smaller, more manageable steps. This approach makes tasks less overwhelming and facilitates steady progress.

Learn to Say No:

- Explanation: Recognize your limits and be selective about taking on additional commitments. Politely decline tasks that may overwhelm your schedule.

Eliminate Time Wasters:

- Explanation: Identify and minimize activities that consume time without contributing to productivity. Limit distractions such as excessive social media use during study sessions.

Practice the Pomodoro Technique:

- Explanation: Break study sessions into intervals, typically 25 minutes of focused work followed by a 5-minute break. This technique enhances concentration and prevents burnout.

Regularly Review and Adjust:

- Explanation: Periodically review your time management strategies to assess their effectiveness. Adjust your approach based on changes in your schedule or workload.

Implementing these time management strategies fosters a balanced and productive approach to academic responsibilities, allowing students to excel academically while maintaining a healthy lifestyle.

6.1.3 Importance of Goal Setting in Academic Success:

- Goal setting is intricately linked to both study skills and time management. CEPRES encourages students to set clear, achievable goals for their academic journey. These goals serve as motivational milestones and provide a roadmap for success.
- By fostering a culture of goal setting, CEPRES helps students stay focused, motivated, and aligned with their academic aspirations.

6.1.3.1 Goal Setting in Academic Success

SETTING ACADEMIC GOALS is a crucial aspect of achieving success in university studies. Goal setting provides a roadmap for students, helping them stay focused, motivated, and organized throughout their academic journey. Here are key aspects of goal setting in academic success:

Clarity and Specificity:

- Explanation: Goals should be clear and specific, outlining exactly what you want to achieve. For example, setting a goal to improve your GPA by 0.5 points is more specific than a vague goal like "get better grades."

Short-Term and Long-Term Goals:

- ***Explanation:*** Divide your academic journey into short-term goals (weekly or monthly) and long-term goals (semester or yearly). Short-term goals help maintain focus, while long-term goals provide a broader perspective.

SMART Criteria:

- ***Explanation:*** Utilize the SMART criteria (Specific, Measurable, Achievable, Relevant, Time-Bound) to structure your goals effectively. This framework ensures that goals are well-defined and attainable.

Self-Monitoring and Reflection:

- ***Explanation***: Regularly monitor your progress toward goals and reflect on your achievements and challenges. Adjust goals as needed based on your evolving understanding of your academic strengths and weaknesses.

Motivation and Intrinsic Rewards:

- ***Explanation***: Understand the intrinsic rewards associated with achieving your academic goals. Connecting goals to personal values and interests enhances motivation, making the pursuit of success more fulfilling.

Flexibility and Adaptability:

- ***Explanation***: Be flexible in adapting your goals to changing circumstances. Academic journeys often involve unexpected challenges, and the ability to adjust goals allows for a more resilient approach to success.

Incorporating these aspects into your goal-setting strategy can contribute significantly to your academic success by providing a structured and motivating framework for your studies.

6.1.4 Effective Note-Taking Strategies:

EFFECTIVE NOTE-TAKING is a critical skill for academic success. It enhances comprehension, aids retention, and provides a valuable resource for exam preparation. Employing the right strategies ensures that your notes are organized, meaningful, and conducive to active learning. Here are key strategies for effective note-taking:

Active Listening:

- ***Explanation***: Actively engage with the lecture or reading material. Listen attentively, identify key points, and focus on the main concepts being discussed.

Use of Abbreviations and Symbols:

- ***Explanation:*** Develop a system of abbreviations and symbols to expedite note-taking. This helps capture information quickly, especially during fast-paced lectures.

Organization and Structuring:

- ***Explanation:*** Adopt a clear organizational structure for your notes. Use headings, bullet points, and numbering to delineate different topics and subtopics.

Visual Aids and Diagrams:

- Explanation: Incorporate visual aids like diagrams, charts, and graphs when applicable. Visual representations can enhance understanding and make complex information more digestible.

Consistency in Format:

- Explanation: Maintain consistency in the format of your notes. A uniform structure makes it easier to review and revise your notes later.

Review and Summarization:

- Explanation: Regularly review and summarize your notes. This not only reinforces learning but also helps identify gaps in your understanding.

Digital Note-Taking Tools:

- Explanation: Explore digital note-taking tools that align with your learning preferences. Platforms like Evernote, OneNote, or tablet apps offer versatility and organization.

Interactive Note-Taking:

- Explanation: Engage with your notes actively. Pose questions, add comments, and make connections between different concepts. This transforms notes into a dynamic learning resource.

Use of Color and Highlighting:

- *Explanation*: Employ color-coding and highlighting to emphasize important points. This visual distinction aids in quick information retrieval.

Collaborative Note-Taking:

- Explanation: Collaborate with peers to enhance note-taking. Discussing and comparing notes can provide different perspectives and fill in gaps in your understanding.

By incorporating these strategies into your note-taking routine, you can optimize your study sessions, reinforce your understanding of course material, and enhance your overall academic performance.

6.1.5 Digital vs. Traditional Note-Taking:

THE CHOICE BETWEEN digital and traditional note-taking methods has become increasingly relevant in today's technology-driven educational landscape. Each approach has its merits and drawbacks, catering to diverse learning preferences and styles. Let's delve into the comparative analysis of digital and traditional note-taking:

6.1.5.1 Accessibility and Portability:

- *Digital*: Digital note-taking offers unparalleled accessibility. Notes stored in the cloud can be accessed from any device with an internet connection, promoting flexibility and convenience.
- *Traditional*: Traditional note-taking relies on physical notebooks, which may be less portable. However, some students appreciate the tactile nature of handwritten notes.

6.1.5.2 Organization and Searchability:

- *Digital:* Digital notes often come with organizational features, enabling easy categorization, tagging, and searchability. This can be a significant advantage when reviewing large volumes of information.
- *Traditional*: Organization in traditional notes depends on the user's manual structuring. Retrieving specific information may be more time-consuming compared to digital methods.

6.1.5.3 Multimodal Content Integration:

- *Digital*: Digital notes allow integration of various media, including images, audio, and video. This feature enhances the depth and richness of notes, accommodating different learning styles.
- *Traditional*: Traditional notes are primarily text-based. While illustrations and diagrams are possible, the process is generally more labor-intensive.

6.1.5.4 Note-Taking Speed:

- *Digital:* Typing can be faster than handwriting for many individuals, especially those proficient in keyboarding. This can be advantageous during fast-paced lectures or when capturing large amounts of information.
- *Traditional*: Handwriting speed varies among individuals. Some may find it challenging to keep up during rapid note-taking situations.

6.1.5.5 Memory Retention and Cognitive Benefits:

- *Digital*: Research suggests that the act of physically writing by hand can enhance memory retention. Some students may find that the tactile experience of writing contributes to better understanding and recall.
- *Traditional:* The kinesthetic aspect of writing on paper can positively impact cognitive processes, fostering a deeper connection to the material.

6.1.5.6 Distraction Level:

- *Digital*: Digital devices, if not used mindfully, can become sources of distraction, with notifications and other apps competing for attention during note-taking.
- *Traditional*: Physical notebooks are generally devoid of external distractions, promoting a more focused and immersive note-taking experience.

6.1.5.7 Battery Dependency:

- *Digital*: Digital devices require power, making users dependent on battery life. Running out of battery during a lecture can disrupt note-taking.
- *Traditional:* Traditional note-taking methods are not subject to battery constraints, ensuring continuous usability.

6.1.5.8 Cost Considerations:

- *Digital*: While there may be an initial investment in digital devices, the cost of digital note-taking apps and cloud storage solutions may be lower in the long run.

- *Traditional:* Traditional note-taking requires notebooks and writing tools, which may incur ongoing costs.

6.1.5.9 Environmental Impact:

- *Digital:* Digital note-taking reduces paper consumption, aligning with eco-friendly practices and minimizing environmental impact.
- *Traditional:* Paper-based note-taking relies on the consumption of physical resources.

IN CONCLUSION, THE choice between digital and traditional note-taking is subjective and depends on individual preferences, learning styles, and the specific requirements of the academic context. Some students may opt for a hybrid approach, combining elements of both methods to leverage the advantages of each. Ultimately, the effectiveness of note-taking lies in how well it aligns with the individual's cognitive processes and enhances the learning experience.

By integrating these elements into the curriculum, CEPRES International University aims to nurture students who not only excel academically but also develop transferable skills that will serve them well in their future professional endeavors. The emphasis on effective study skills and time management reflects the institution's commitment to holistic education and the success of its students beyond the classroom.

6.2 Goal Setting:

GOAL SETTING IS A FUNDAMENTAL component of academic success and personal development at CEPRES International University. Dr. Mogana S. Flomo, Jr., the visionary founder of CEPRES, recognizes the transformative power of clear goals in shaping students' educational journeys. Here, we delve into the discussion of goal setting and its significance within the context of CEPRES International University:

6.2.1 Alignment with Academic Aspirations:

ACHIEVING ACADEMIC success requires a deliberate alignment with one's academic aspirations. This process involves setting clear goals, developing effective strategies, and maintaining a focused approach. The significance of aligning actions with academic aspirations is paramount for students pursuing excellence. Let's explore this concept in detail:

6.2.1.1 Clarity in Goal Setting:

IDENTIFICATION OF ACADEMIC Objectives:

Students should articulate their academic aspirations by defining specific, measurable, achievable, relevant, and time-bound (SMART) goals. These objectives may include academic achievements, skill development, or personal growth.

6.2.1.2 Motivation and Commitment:

INTRINSIC MOTIVATION*:*

Aligning actions with academic aspirations fosters intrinsic motivation. When students recognize the relevance of their efforts to their long-term goals, they are more likely to remain committed and persevere through challenges.

6.2.1.3 Academic Planning and Strategy:

STRATEGIC ACADEMIC Planning:

Students must create a roadmap that outlines the steps needed to achieve their academic aspirations. This may involve developing a study schedule, setting milestones, and utilizing resources effectively.

6.2.1.4 Utilization of Educational Resources:

LEVERAGING ACADEMIC Resources:
Aligning with academic aspirations involves identifying and utilizing available resources, such as libraries, online databases, academic support services, and faculty guidance. Maximizing these resources enhances the learning experience.

6.2.1.5 Skill Development and Specialization:

BUILDING RELEVANT SKILLS:
Academic aspirations often involve acquiring specific skills related to a chosen field of study. Students should focus on skill development through coursework, projects, internships, and extracurricular activities aligned with their academic goals.

6.2.1.6 Continuous Learning and Adaptability:

EMBRACING A GROWTH Mindset:
Alignment with academic aspirations requires a growth mindset that embraces challenges and views setbacks as opportunities for learning. This mindset promotes continuous learning and adaptability to evolving academic demands.

6.2.1.7 Time Management and Prioritization:

EFFECTIVE TIME ALLOCATION:

Students need to manage their time efficiently, prioritizing activities that directly contribute to their academic goals. This includes balancing coursework, research, and personal commitments.

6.2.1.8 Networking and Collaboration:

BUILDING ACADEMIC CONNECTIONS:
Aligning with academic aspirations involves connecting with peers, faculty, and professionals in the chosen field. Networking facilitates collaboration, knowledge sharing, and opportunities for academic and career growth.

6.2.1.9 Reflective Practices:

REGULAR SELF-REFLECTION:
Students should engage in regular self-reflection to assess their progress, identify areas for improvement, and adjust their strategies accordingly. This reflective practice enhances self-awareness and goal alignment.

6.2.1.10 Integration of Extracurricular Activities:

BALANCING ACADEMICS and Well-Rounded Development:
Aligning with academic aspirations goes beyond coursework. Involvement in extracurricular activities, leadership roles, and community service contributes to holistic development, aligning with broader educational goals.

6.2.1.11 Evaluation of Academic Choices:

ASSESSMENT OF ACADEMIC Decisions:

Students should periodically evaluate their academic choices, ensuring that courses, majors, and research align with their evolving aspirations. This evaluation enables informed decision-making.

In summary, alignment with academic aspirations is a dynamic and intentional process that involves goal setting, strategic planning, skill development, and continuous self-reflection. By maintaining this alignment, students cultivate a purposeful academic journey that not only leads to success in the short term but also prepares them for long-term achievements in their chosen fields.

6.2.2 Motivational Milestones:

IN THE PURSUIT OF ACADEMIC success, CEPRES acknowledges the profound impact of setting and achieving motivational milestones. These milestones, often comprised of smaller, incremental goals, play a pivotal role in shaping students' academic journeys. Let's delve into the significance of these motivational milestones and their transformative effects on students:

6.2.2.1 Setting Clear Objectives:

CLARITY IN GOAL SETTING:

Motivational milestones begin with the establishment of clear and attainable objectives. CEPRES encourages students to set specific, measurable, and realistic goals that align with their academic aspirations.

6.2.2.2 Incremental Achievements:

BUILDING BLOCK APPROACH:

Recognizing that large goals can be overwhelming, CEPRES promotes a building block approach. Students are encouraged to break down their academic aspirations into smaller, manageable tasks, creating a series of incremental achievements.

6.2.2.3 Enhancing Confidence Levels:

CELEBRATING SMALL WINS:
As students accomplish these smaller goals, they experience a sense of accomplishment. Celebrating these victories, no matter how modest, contributes to a positive reinforcement loop, boosting confidence levels and reinforcing a proactive mindset.

6.2.2.4 Creating Momentum:

PROPELLING TOWARD LARGER Goals:
Each achieved milestone generates momentum. Students find themselves propelled forward by a sense of achievement, motivating them to tackle more substantial challenges with increased vigor and determination.

6.2.2.5 Positive Feedback Loop:

FEEDBACK AS A MOTIVATOR:
The positive feedback loop created by accomplishing milestones serves as a powerful motivator. Recognizing one's capabilities and the impact of effort fosters a positive mindset, encouraging students to persist in the face of challenges.

6.2.2.6 Cultivating Resilience:

LEARNING FROM CHALLENGES:
Not every endeavor unfolds seamlessly. CEPRES emphasizes that encountering challenges is an integral part of the learning process.

Through overcoming obstacles, students develop resilience and learn valuable lessons that contribute to their personal and academic growth.

6.2.2.7 Fostering Intrinsic Motivation:

INTERNAL DRIVE FOR Success:

Motivational milestones contribute to the development of intrinsic motivation. Students begin to derive satisfaction from the pursuit of knowledge and personal growth, fostering a sustainable drive that extends beyond external recognition.

6.2.2.8 Goal Refinement and Adaptability:

ITERATIVE GOAL-SETTING Process:

Achieving motivational milestones provides students with insights into their strengths and areas for improvement. This iterative process allows for the refinement of goals and strategies, fostering adaptability in the pursuit of academic success.

6.2.2.9 Building a Positive Mindset:

SHAPING A PROACTIVE Mindset:

Consistent success in reaching milestones shapes a positive mindset. Students come to view challenges as opportunities for growth and learning, cultivating a proactive approach to their academic endeavors.

6.2.2.10 Long-Term Impact:

FOUNDATION FOR SIGNIFICANT Achievements:

Motivational milestones serve as a foundation for more significant accomplishments. By instilling a sense of efficacy and perseverance, students are better equipped to tackle complex challenges and pursue long-term academic goals.

In summary, CEPRES recognizes that the journey to academic success is punctuated by motivational milestones. These incremental achievements contribute to the development of confidence, resilience, and intrinsic motivation, creating a positive feedback loop that propels students towards greater accomplishments. By celebrating each step forward, students cultivate a mindset that not only fosters success in the present but also lays the groundwork for a fulfilling academic future.

6.2.3 Practical Goal-Setting Approaches:

IN THE PURSUIT OF ACADEMIC excellence, CEPRES recognizes the pivotal role that effective goal setting plays in guiding students towards success. The institution emphasizes practical approaches to goal setting, placing a strong emphasis on the SMART criteria—Specific, Measurable, Achievable, Relevant, and Time-Bound. Let's explore how CEPRES encourages students to adopt these practical goal-setting approaches:

6.2.3.1 Specific Goals:

CLEAR AND WELL-DEFINED Objectives:
CEPRES underscores the importance of specificity in goal setting. Students are encouraged to articulate precisely what they aim to achieve. Specific goals provide clarity, reducing ambiguity and enhancing focus.

6.2.3.2 Measurable Outcomes:

QUANTIFIABLE PROGRESS Indicators:

Measurability is crucial for tracking progress. CEPRES advises students to establish clear metrics or indicators that allow for the quantitative assessment of their advancements. Measurable outcomes enable students to gauge their success and adjust their strategies accordingly.

6.2.3.3 Achievable Targets:

REALISTIC AND ATTAINABLE Milestones:
Goals should challenge individuals to grow while remaining within feasibility. CEPRES promotes the setting of achievable targets, ensuring that students are neither overwhelmed by the magnitude of their aspirations nor confined by excessively modest objectives.

6.2.3.4 Relevance to Aspirations:

ALIGNMENT WITH ACADEMIC and Personal Objectives:
For goals to be meaningful, they must align with the broader aspirations of students. CEPRES encourages learners to assess the relevance of their goals to their academic journey and personal development, fostering a sense of purpose and motivation.

6.2.3.5 Time-Bound Framework:

ESTABLISHMENT OF CLEAR Timeframes:
Time constraints provide structure and urgency. CEPRES advises students to set specific deadlines for the attainment of their goals, instilling a sense of accountability and preventing procrastination.

6.2.3.6 Preventing Overwhelm:

BREAKING DOWN LARGER Goals:

CEPRES acknowledges that substantial goals can be daunting. By breaking down overarching objectives into smaller, manageable tasks, students can prevent feelings of overwhelm. This incremental approach facilitates steady progress and enhances motivation.

6.2.3.7 Flexibility and Adaptability:

ITERATIVE GOAL REFINEMENT:

Practical goal setting is not a rigid process. CEPRES encourages students to periodically review and refine their goals based on evolving circumstances. This adaptive approach ensures that goals remain relevant and realistic amid changing academic and personal landscapes.

6.2.3.8 Visualizing Success:

ENCOURAGING POSITIVE Visualization:

Visualization is a powerful tool in goal setting. CEPRES advises students to vividly imagine themselves achieving their goals. This positive visualization enhances motivation, fosters a positive mindset, and reinforces the belief in one's capabilities.

6.2.3.9 Feedback and Reflection:

CONTINUOUS ASSESSMENT and Reflection:

Goal setting is an iterative process. CEPRES encourages students to regularly assess their progress, seek feedback, and reflect on their experiences. This ongoing evaluation allows for adjustments, learning from setbacks, and celebrating successes.

6.2.3.10 Integration with Academic Journey:

HARMONIZING GOALS WITH Academic Pathway:

CEPRES emphasizes that goals should complement the broader academic journey. Practical goal setting involves aligning short-term objectives with long-term aspirations, ensuring a cohesive and purpose-driven educational experience.

In summary, CEPRES fosters practical goal-setting approaches centered around the SMART criteria. By guiding students to craft goals that are Specific, Measurable, Achievable, Relevant, and Time-Bound, the institution empowers learners to navigate their academic journeys with clarity, motivation, and a strategic mindset.

6.2.4 Individualized Goal Setting:

RECOGNIZING THE UNIQUE and diverse aspirations of its student body, CEPRES champions the philosophy of individualized goal setting. In contrast to a one-size-fits-all approach, the institution encourages students to embark on a reflective journey that considers their distinctive strengths, interests, and values. This commitment to individualized goal setting is underpinned by several key principles:

6.2.4.1 Personal Reflection:

UNDERSTANDING PERSONAL Strengths:
CEPRES guides students in introspective reflections to discern their individual strengths. By recognizing and leveraging these strengths, students can tailor their goals to align with their innate capabilities and talents.

6.2.4.2 Interest-Based Goals:

ALIGNING WITH PASSIONATE Pursuits:
The institution emphasizes the importance of aligning goals with students' interests. By pursuing objectives that resonate with their

passions, learners are more likely to stay motivated and engaged throughout their academic journey.

6.2.4.3 Values as Guideposts:

INCORPORATING PERSONAL Values:
CEPRES encourages students to integrate their personal values into their goal-setting process. This values-driven approach ensures that the pursuit of goals is not only academically meaningful but also aligned with students' ethical and moral principles.

6.2.4.4 Tailored Milestones:

CRAFTING GOALS TO SUIT Individual Capacities:
Individualized goal setting involves tailoring milestones to suit each student's unique capacities. By acknowledging personal limitations and growth areas, learners can set realistic yet challenging objectives that promote continuous improvement.

6.2.4.5 Authentic Aspirations:

FOSTERING AUTHENTIC Goal-Setting:
CEPRES instills the belief that goals should authentically reflect the aspirations of each student. By promoting authenticity in goal setting, the institution aims to cultivate a genuine commitment to personal and academic growth.

6.2.4.6 Ownership of Objectives:

EMPOWERING STUDENTS through Ownership:
Individualized goal setting empowers students to take ownership of their academic journey. CEPRES believes that when learners actively

shape their goals, they develop a sense of responsibility and accountability for their educational outcomes.

6.2.4.7 Flexible Pathways:

ADAPTING GOALS TO INDIVIDUAL Trajectories:
CEPRES recognizes that individual trajectories vary. The institution encourages students to adapt their goals in response to changing circumstances, fostering flexibility and resilience in the face of academic challenges.

6.2.4.8 Mental and Emotional Well-being:

PRIORITIZING PERSONAL Well-being:
Beyond academic achievements, individualized goal setting at CEPRES takes into account students' mental and emotional well-being. Goals are crafted with consideration for maintaining a healthy balance between academic pursuits and personal happiness.

6.2.4.9 Long-Term Vision:

ALIGNING SHORT-TERM Goals with Long-Term Vision:
CEPRES facilitates a holistic approach to goal setting by guiding students to align short-term objectives with their long-term vision. This strategic alignment ensures coherence in their academic and personal development.

6.2.4.10 Cultivating Lifelong Learners:

FOSTERING A LIFELONG Learning Mindset:
Individualized goal setting contributes to the cultivation of lifelong learners. By tailoring goals to individual interests and strengths,

CEPRES aims to instill a passion for continuous learning beyond the confines of formal education.

In summary, CEPRES's commitment to individualized goal setting reflects a dedication to recognizing and honoring the diverse pathways students may tread on their academic journey. Through this approach, the institution aims to empower learners to set goals that resonate with their unique identities, fostering a genuine and enduring commitment to personal and academic growth.

6.2.5 Integration into Academic and Personal Development:

AT CEPRES, THE PHILOSOPHY of goal setting extends beyond the academic realm, becoming an integral part of students' holistic development. The institution believes that effective goal setting should not be confined to academic achievements alone but should encompass personal growth, ethical development, and preparation for future professional roles. This commitment is reflected in several key aspects:

6.2.5.1 Academic Excellence:

STRIVING FOR SCHOLARLY Success:

CEPRES encourages students to set academic goals that go beyond mere grades. Whether aiming for research excellence, active participation in class discussions, or mastering specific subjects, academic goals are seen as contributors to broader intellectual development.

6.2.5.2 Research and Innovation:

SETTING AMBITIOUS RESEARCH Goals:

For students engaged in research projects, goal setting becomes a tool for driving innovation. CEPRES guides individuals to articulate goals that challenge existing boundaries, fostering a culture of intellectual curiosity and breakthrough discoveries.

6.2.5.3 Community Engagement:

GOALS ALIGNED WITH Social Impact:
Recognizing the importance of social responsibility, CEPRES integrates community service goals into students' developmental plans. Whether through environmental initiatives, health promotion projects, or other community-focused endeavors, students set goals that contribute to societal well-being.

6.2.5.4 Professional Development:

PREPARING FOR FUTURE Roles:
CEPRES views goal setting as a means of preparing students for their future professional roles. Goals related to internships, industry exposure, and skill development are aligned with the institution's vision of producing graduates who are not only academically proficient but also well-prepared for the demands of their chosen professions.

6.2.5.5 Ethical Growth:

GUIDING GOALS FOR ETHICAL Development:
CEPRES recognizes the importance of ethical considerations in personal and professional life. Goal setting includes objectives related to ethical decision-making, social responsibility, and the development of a strong moral compass.

6.2.5.6 Interdisciplinary Perspectives:

FOSTERING WELL-ROUNDED Individuals:

The integration of academic and personal development goals emphasizes the importance of interdisciplinary perspectives. Students are encouraged to set goals that span diverse fields, promoting a well-rounded education that extends beyond traditional disciplinary boundaries.

6.2.5.7 Leadership and Initiative:

EMPOWERING GOAL SETTING for Leadership:

Aspiring to nurture future leaders, CEPRES guides students in setting goals that enhance leadership skills. Whether through involvement in student organizations, leading projects, or initiating positive changes, goals are aligned with the development of leadership qualities.

6.2.5.8 Reflective Practices:

GOAL SETTING AS A REFLECTIVE Process:

CEPRES emphasizes the reflective aspect of goal setting. Students are encouraged to regularly review and adjust their goals in response to evolving personal and academic contexts, fostering a continuous cycle of self-improvement.

6.2.5.9 Mental and Emotional Well-being:

BALANCING ACADEMIC and Personal Goals:

CEPRES acknowledges the importance of mental and emotional well-being. Goal setting includes objectives aimed at maintaining a healthy balance between academic pursuits and personal happiness, fostering resilient and fulfilled individuals.

6.2.5.10 Preparation for Lifelong Learning:

EMBEDDING A LIFELONG Learning Mindset:

By integrating goal setting into both academic and personal realms, CEPRES aims to instill a mindset of lifelong learning. Goals become not just milestones but continuous guides in the journey towards becoming informed, ethical, and adaptable lifelong learners.

In essence, the integration of goal setting into academic and personal development at CEPRES underscores the institution's commitment to nurturing well-rounded individuals. By guiding students to set goals that contribute to academic excellence, social impact, ethical growth, and professional preparedness, CEPRES strives to cultivate graduates who are not only successful in their careers but also conscientious contributors to society.

6.2.6 Reflection and Adaptation:

AT CEPRES, THE JOURNEY of goal setting extends beyond mere establishment; it embodies a dynamic and iterative process grounded in regular reflection and adaptation. The institution recognizes that the pursuit of personal and academic goals is a fluid and evolving experience, requiring students to engage in deliberate introspection and make adjustments as needed. This commitment to reflective practices is evident in several key dimensions:

6.2.6.1 Progress Assessment:

CELEBRATING MILESTONES:

CEPRES encourages students to regularly assess their progress toward established goals. Acknowledging and celebrating even the smallest milestones fosters a positive mindset and fuels motivation for the ongoing journey.

6.2.6.2 Self-Reflection:

INTERNALIZING ACHIEVEMENTS and Challenges:

The reflective process involves deep self-reflection. Students are guided to internalize both their achievements and challenges, gaining insights into their strengths, areas for improvement, and the factors influencing their goal pursuit.

6.2.6.3 Adaptation to Evolving Circumstances:

FLEXIBILITY IN GOAL Setting:

CEPRES emphasizes the importance of flexibility in goal setting. Recognizing that circumstances may change, students are empowered to adapt their goals to align with evolving personal, academic, or external factors.

6.2.6.4 Guidance and Mentorship:

SUPPORTING THROUGH Guidance:

The university provides a supportive environment for reflection by offering guidance and mentorship. Students have access to resources and advisors who assist them in navigating challenges, making informed decisions, and refining their goals.

6.2.6.5 Strategic Adjustments:

MAKING INFORMED CHANGES:

Reflective practices involve making strategic adjustments to goals. Whether refining objectives, modifying timelines, or exploring new aspirations, students are encouraged to make informed changes that align with their evolving aspirations.

6.2.6.6 Learning from Setbacks:

TURNING CHALLENGES into Opportunities:
Setbacks are viewed not as failures but as opportunities for learning and growth. CEPRES promotes a mindset that sees challenges as integral parts of the journey, providing valuable lessons that contribute to resilience and adaptability.

6.2.6.7 Peer Collaboration:

SHARED LEARNING AND Insights:
Reflective practices extend to collaborative learning among peers. Students are encouraged to share their reflections, insights, and strategies for goal achievement, fostering a sense of community and shared learning.

6.2.6.8 Long-Term Vision:

ALIGNING SHORT-TERM Goals with Long-Term Vision:
The reflective process involves aligning short-term goals with the overarching long-term vision. This approach ensures that each milestone contributes meaningfully to the broader educational and personal journey.

6.2.6.9 Cultivation of Growth Mindset:

EMBRACING A GROWTH Mindset:
CEPRES instills a growth mindset, emphasizing that abilities can be developed through dedication and hard work. The reflective process reinforces this mindset, positioning challenges as opportunities for growth rather than insurmountable obstacles.

6.2.6.10 Empowerment Through Ownership:

TAKING OWNERSHIP OF the Journey:
By encouraging regular reflection, CEPRES empowers students to take ownership of their academic and personal journey. The ability to critically evaluate their goals, make adjustments, and set new objectives cultivates a sense of agency and responsibility.

In essence, the emphasis on reflection and adaptation at CEPRES embodies a commitment to holistic student development. By fostering an environment where continuous self-assessment is valued and supported, the university aims to cultivate individuals who not only achieve their goals but also evolve into adaptive, resilient, and reflective lifelong learners.

6.2.7 Cultivation of Lifelong Learning Habits:

AT CEPRES, THE COMMITMENT to student development extends far beyond the academic journey within the university's walls. Recognizing that education is a lifelong endeavor, the institution places a significant emphasis on cultivating habits of continuous learning. The cultivation of lifelong learning habits serves as a cornerstone of the educational philosophy at CEPRES, and several key principles underscore this commitment:

6.2.7.1 Integration of Goal Setting and Lifelong Learning:

SEAMLESS TRANSITION:
CEPRES integrates goal setting seamlessly with the concept of lifelong learning. Goals are not viewed in isolation but as interconnected milestones contributing to an individual's ongoing educational and personal development.

6.2.7.2 Skill Development for Adaptability:

PREPARATION FOR THE Future:
The skills acquired through goal setting at CEPRES go beyond achieving specific objectives within the university context. Students are equipped with adaptability, resilience, and a growth mindset—attributes crucial for navigating the ever-evolving landscape of knowledge and skills in their future endeavors.

6.2.7.3 Encouragement of Inquisitiveness:

FUELING CURIOSITY:
Lifelong learners possess an innate inquisitiveness. CEPRES fosters an environment that encourages students to remain curious and motivated to explore new domains of knowledge even after completing their formal education.

6.2.7.4 Continuous Skill Refinement:

ADAPTING TO CHANGES:
As the professional landscape evolves, so do the skills required for success. Lifelong learning habits involve the continuous refinement and acquisition of skills to stay relevant and effective in an ever-changing world.

6.2.7.5 Emphasis on Critical Thinking:

BEYOND MEMORIZATION:
Lifelong learning extends beyond memorization. CEPRES emphasizes critical thinking skills, empowering students to analyze, synthesize, and apply information—essential abilities for individuals committed to ongoing intellectual growth.

6.2.7.6 Resource Access Beyond Graduation:

ALUMNI RESOURCES:
CEPRES extends access to resources and support beyond graduation. Alumni are provided with opportunities to continue their education, access updated materials, and engage with the university community, reinforcing the notion that learning is a lifelong pursuit.

6.2.7.7 Adoption of New Technologies:

EMBRACING TECHNOLOGICAL Advances:
Lifelong learners are adept at embracing new technologies. CEPRES ensures that students are not only familiar with current technologies but are also prepared to adapt to emerging innovations, enabling them to thrive in a technology-driven world.

6.2.7.8 Professional Development Opportunities:

SUPPORT FOR CAREER Advancement:
Lifelong learning habits contribute to professional development. CEPRES provides avenues for alumni to engage in continuous learning related to their professions, fostering career advancement and expertise enhancement.

6.2.7.9 Community of Learners:

NETWORKING FOR KNOWLEDGE Exchange:
CEPRES promotes a sense of community among its learners, even after graduation. Lifelong learners are encouraged to connect with fellow alumni, faculty, and industry professionals, fostering a network for ongoing knowledge exchange.

6.2.7.10 Global Perspectives:

EMBRACING DIVERSITY of Thought:

Lifelong learners appreciate diverse perspectives. CEPRES instills a global outlook, preparing students to seek knowledge from various sources, embrace diversity of thought, and apply their learning in a global context.

In essence, the cultivation of lifelong learning habits at CEPRES reflects a commitment to nurturing individuals who not only excel academically but also embark on a journey of continuous intellectual, personal, and professional growth. The goal-setting practices ingrained in students during their

university years serve as the foundation for a mindset that values learning as a lifelong pursuit. By instilling this philosophy, CEPRES aims to empower its graduates to navigate the complexities of the future with curiosity, adaptability, and a passion for continuous self-improvement.

In conclusion, CEPRES International University views goal setting as an integral aspect of cultivating success-oriented mindsets among its students. By fostering a culture of purposeful goal setting, the university contributes to the holistic development of individuals who are not only academically proficient but also equipped with the skills to navigate challenges and seize opportunities in their future endeavors.

6.3 Effective Note-Taking Strategies:

EFFECTIVE NOTE-TAKING is a cornerstone of academic success, and CEPRES International University places a strong emphasis on equipping students with robust strategies to enhance their learning experience. Dr. Mogana S. Flomo, Jr., the visionary founder of CEPRES, recognizes the transformative impact of effective note-taking in promoting comprehension and retention. Here, we delve into the discussion of note-taking strategies and their significance within the context of CEPRES International University:

6.3.1 Note-Taking Methods:

IN THE PURSUIT OF ACADEMIC excellence, note-taking stands out as a fundamental skill that students at CEPRES are encouraged to master. Recognizing the diverse learning styles and preferences of its students, the university advocates for a variety of note-taking methods. These methods are tailored to suit different contexts, subjects, and individual preferences. Below are some key note-taking methods emphasized at CEPRES:

6.3.1.1 Cornell Method:

- *Structured Approach*: The Cornell Method provides a structured and systematic format for organizing notes. Students divide their notes into sections for cues, main ideas, and summaries, enhancing the organization and retrieval of information.
- *Active Engagement*: Encouraging active engagement, this method prompts students to reflect on and summarize the material during the note-taking process, fostering deeper understanding

6.3.1.2 Mapping Approach:

- *Visual Representation*: The Mapping Approach involves creating visual representations of concepts and their relationships. It utilizes diagrams, flowcharts, and mind maps to convey information in a visually engaging manner.
- *Enhanced Creativity*: Particularly effective for visual learners, this method enhances creativity and aids in grasping complex

relationships between ideas.

6.3.1.3 Linear Note-Taking:

- *Sequential Structure*: Linear note-taking follows a sequential structure, with information presented in a chronological or ordered fashion. This method is straightforward and effective for subjects with a clear progression of ideas.
- *Simplicity and Clarity*: Linear notes are concise and easy to review, making them suitable for capturing essential points during lectures or readings.

6.3.1.4 Outline Method:

HIERARCHICAL STRUCTURE: The Outline Method organizes information hierarchically, with main topics and subtopics arranged in a systematic outline format. It emphasizes the relationships between different levels of information.

Logical Organization: Ideal for subjects with a hierarchical structure, this method supports logical organization and aids in the identification of key concepts.

6.3.1.5 Charting Method:

- *Tabular Representation*: The Charting Method involves creating tables or charts to categorize and compare information. It is particularly effective for subjects requiring the comparison of different attributes or characteristics.
- *Facilitates Comparison*: This method facilitates a quick overview of information, making it valuable for summarizing and comparing data.

6.3.1.6 Sentence Method:

- *Complete Sentences*: The Sentence Method involves writing complete sentences to capture information. This approach is beneficial for detailed and comprehensive note-taking, especially in subjects that require capturing nuanced explanations.
- *Facilitates Review*: The use of complete sentences makes the notes self-contained and facilitates easier review of the material.

EACH OF THESE NOTE-taking methods aligns with the diverse learning needs of students at CEPRES, offering flexibility based on the nature of the content and individual preferences. The emphasis on a range of methods reflects the university's commitment to providing students with the tools they need to succeed academically and develop effective study habits.

6.3.2 Active Engagement with Course Materials:

- The university emphasizes that effective note-taking goes beyond passive transcription. Students are encouraged to engage actively with course materials, identifying key concepts, relationships, and practical applications. This approach transforms notes into valuable study resources.

6.3.3 Customization for Individual Learning Styles:

- Recognizing that students have unique learning styles, CEPRES supports customization in note-taking. Whether through mind maps, outlines, charts, or Cornell note-taking systems, students are guided to adopt methods that resonate with their individual preferences and optimize information retention.

6.3.4 Digital vs. Traditional Note-Taking:

- Acknowledging the technological landscape, CEPRES provides comprehensive guidance on both digital and traditional note-taking. Students learn to leverage digital tools for organization, collaboration, and accessibility, while also appreciating the tactile benefits of traditional note-taking methods.

6.3.5 Integration of Multimedia Elements:

- CEPRES encourages students to enhance their notes with multimedia elements. Integrating visual aids, diagrams, and audio recordings enriches the note-taking process, catering to different learning modalities and reinforcing understanding.

6.3.6 Strategic Use of Annotations and Highlights:

- The university teaches students to strategically use annotations and highlights in their notes. This targeted approach helps emphasize key points, draw connections, and streamline the review process, particularly during exam preparation.

6.3.7 Synthesis and Summarization:

- CEPRES fosters note-taking practices that involve synthesis and summarization. Students learn to distill complex information into concise summaries, reinforcing their understanding of core concepts and facilitating efficient review sessions.

6.3.8 Collaborative Note-Taking:

- Recognizing the value of collaboration, CEPRES promotes collaborative note-taking. Whether through group discussions or shared digital platforms, students have the opportunity to benefit from diverse perspectives, fill gaps in their understanding, and collectively create comprehensive study materials.

6.3.9 Time Management during Note-Taking:

- Efficient time management during lectures and study sessions is integral to effective note-taking. CEPRES provides strategies for students to prioritize information, identify key takeaways, and streamline the note-taking process without sacrificing depth of understanding.

6.3.10 Continuous Improvement and Reflection:

- CEPRES encourages students to view note-taking as a skill that evolves over time. Regular reflection on note-taking practices, seeking feedback, and making adjustments based on individual learning experiences contribute to continuous improvement.

BY INTEGRATING THESE effective note-taking strategies into the curriculum, CEPRES International University aims to empower students with skills that extend beyond the classroom. The emphasis on active engagement, customization, and continuous improvement reflects the institution's commitment to fostering independent, resourceful learners ready to excel in their academic and professional pursuits.

7 Introduction to Basic Computer Skills

7.1 Operating Systems Overview

WELCOME TO THE COMPREHENSIVE module on "Operating Systems Overview" at CEPRES International University. In this session, we will delve into the fundamental concepts of operating systems, laying the groundwork for a deeper understanding of how these systems function within computing. CEPRES, recognizes the pivotal role of operating systems in modern computing and aims to equip students with essential knowledge in this domain.

7.1.1 Understanding Operating Systems:

DEFINITION AND PURPOSE:

An operating system (OS) serves as the core software that manages computer hardware and provides essential services for computer programs. It acts as an intermediary between users and the computer hardware, ensuring efficient and secure execution of applications.

Key Functions of Operating Systems:

- ***Process Management***: Controlling and executing processes within the computer.
- ***Memory Management***: Allocating and managing computer memory.
- ***File System Management***: Organizing and storing files on storage devices.
- ***Device Management***: Managing input and output devices.
- ***Security and Access Control***: Ensuring system security and regulating user access.

7.1.2 Types of Operating Systems:

IN OPERATING SYSTEMS, the distinction between different types plays a pivotal role in aligning technology with user requirements. Here, we explore key types, shedding light on their characteristics and applications:

7.1.2.1 Single-User vs. Multi-User Operating Systems:

- *Single-User*: Designed for a solo user, this type caters to personal computers where one user interacts with the system at a time.
- *Multi-User*: Tailored for scenarios where multiple users access the system concurrently, common in networked environments or servers.

7.1.2.2 Single-Tasking vs. Multi-Tasking Operating Systems:

- *Single-Tasking*: Executes one task at a time, ideal for simpler systems or those with limited resources where focusing on one task enhances efficiency.
- *Multi-Tasking*: Handles multiple tasks simultaneously, prevalent in modern operating systems, enabling users to run various applications concurrently for enhanced productivity.

7.1.2.3 Batch Processing vs. Interactive Systems:

- *Batch Processing*: Involves processing a set of tasks without user intervention. It's suited for scenarios where tasks can be executed sequentially without requiring immediate user input.
- *Interactive Systems*: Facilitates user interaction during task execution, allowing real-time input and feedback. Common

in desktop environments and systems where user engagement is essential.

UNDERSTANDING THESE distinctions is essential for selecting an operating system that aligns with specific use cases. For instance, a single-user, single-tasking system might be suitable for basic personal computing, while a multi-user, multi-tasking system is essential for complex, networked environments. Batch processing finds its application in scenarios where tasks can be automated and processed in batches without constant supervision, whereas interactive systems are crucial for real-time user engagement and feedback.

In summary, the types of operating systems play a crucial role in determining how computers function and cater to user needs. Whether it's a single-user system for personal use, a multi-user system for collaborative work, a single-tasking system for efficiency, or a multi-tasking system for productivity, the right choice depends on the specific requirements and functionalities desired by users and organizations.

7.1.3 Overview of Popular Operating Systems:

IN THE DIVERSE LANDSCAPE of operating systems, several giants stand out, each catering to distinct preferences and functionalities. Let's take a journey through some of the most prominent ones:

7.1.3.1 Windows:

Figure 12: Microsoft Windows Icon

DEVELOPED BY MICROSOFT, Windows is a household name in personal computing and corporate environments. Renowned for its user-friendly interface, Windows operates on a vast array of hardware and supports an extensive range of applications. Its versatility and compatibility make it a popular choice for users spanning from casual home users to large enterprises.

7.1.3.2 MacOS:

Figure 13: MacOS Icon

EXCLUSIVE TO APPLE hardware, MacOS is the epitome of sleek design and seamless integration. Favored by creative professionals, MacOS provides an aesthetically pleasing and efficient environment. The marriage of MacOS with Apple's line of devices ensures a cohesive user experience, making it a top choice for those deeply entrenched in the Apple ecosystem.

7.1.3.3 Linux:

Figure 14: Linux OS Icon

EMBODYING THE SPIRIT of open-source innovation, Linux has found its niche in servers and embedded systems. Boasting high customization options, Linux is recognized for its stability and security features. Its open nature encourages collaboration and has led to various distributions tailored to diverse user preferences. Linux is a preferred choice for those seeking flexibility and control over their operating system.

7.1.3.4 Android and iOS:

IN THE MOBILE DOMAIN, Android and iOS reign supreme. Android, developed by Google, and iOS, exclusive to Apple devices, power the majority of smartphones and tablets. These operating systems bring forth unique user experiences and vibrant app ecosystems. Android, known for its openness and adaptability, caters to a wide range of devices, while iOS, with its curated environment, is synonymous with a premium mobile experience.

As we navigate the digital landscape, these operating systems play a crucial role in shaping our interactions with technology. From the ubiquitous Windows powering our PCs to the elegant MacOS enhancing creative endeavors, and the versatile Linux offering flexibility, to the dynamic Android and iOS driving our mobile experiences, each system contributes to the diverse tapestry of the digital world.

7.1.4 Operating System Components:

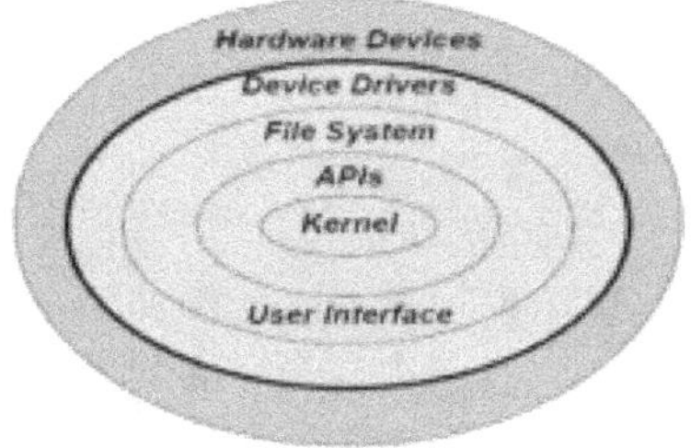

Figure 15:(*Components of Operating System Image - Google Search*, n.d.)

WITHIN THE INTRICATE architecture of an operating system lie key components, each playing a pivotal role in orchestrating the symphony of interactions between software and hardware. Let's delve into the fundamental elements that constitute the backbone of an operating system:

7.1.4.1 Kernel:

AT THE HEART OF EVERY operating system resides the kernel, a paramount component responsible for managing hardware resources. This core entity facilitates seamless communication between software applications and the underlying hardware. It undertakes critical tasks such as process management, memory allocation, and device communication, ensuring the coordinated functioning of the entire system.

7.1.4.2 Shell

SERVING AS THE INTERMEDIARY between users and the operating system, the shell provides the interface through which users interact with the system. Users communicate commands to the operating system via the shell, which interprets and executes these commands. The shell's significance lies in its ability to translate human-readable commands into instructions that the kernel comprehends, thus enabling users to navigate and control the system effectively.

7.1.4.3 Device Drivers:

ENABLING A HARMONIOUS connection between the operating system and hardware devices, device drivers act as specialized software modules. These drivers serve as interpreters, facilitating communication between the operating system and diverse hardware components like printers, keyboards, graphics cards, and more. By abstracting the complexity of hardware interactions, device drivers ensure that the operating system can effectively utilize and manage various peripherals.

In essence, the kernel, shell, and device drivers form the triad that empowers an operating system to function as a cohesive and responsive entity. The kernel manages the core operations, the shell provides a user-friendly interface, and device drivers facilitate seamless communication with the hardware. Together, these components create a dynamic environment where software and hardware collaborate to execute the myriad tasks demanded by users.

This Operating Systems Overview module serves as a foundational exploration into the world of operating systems. As we progress through this course, you will gain deeper insights into specific operating systems, their functionalities, and practical applications.

CIU envisions that this knowledge will empower you to navigate the digital landscape with confidence and contribute meaningfully to the field of computer science and technology. Let's embark on this learning journey together!

7.2 File Management Basics

WELCOME TO THE MODULE on "File Management Basics" at CEPRES International University. In this session, we will explore the essential concepts of file management, an integral aspect of operating systems. CIU recognizes the importance of efficient file management in organizing and accessing digital information, and this module aims to equip you with the foundational knowledge in this area.

7.2.1 Understanding File Management:

IN OPERATING SYSTEMS, file management stands as a cornerstone, orchestrating the organization, storage, and retrieval of digital data. This system plays a crucial role in maintaining order within the digital landscape, allowing users to interact seamlessly with their files. Let's explore the fundamentals of file management:

7.2.1.1 Definition and Purpose:

AT ITS CORE, FILE MANAGEMENT is the systematic handling of digital data. Operating systems employ file management systems to impose structure on the myriad files users generate, ensuring accessibility, organization, and ease of use. The overarching purpose is to streamline the user experience, making it efficient to create, locate, modify, and store digital information.

7.2.1.2 Hierarchy of Data Organization:

FILES:

These are the elemental units of digital data, encompassing a diverse array of information such as documents, images, spreadsheets, and more. Files serve as the building blocks of digital content, each carrying its own distinct purpose and format.

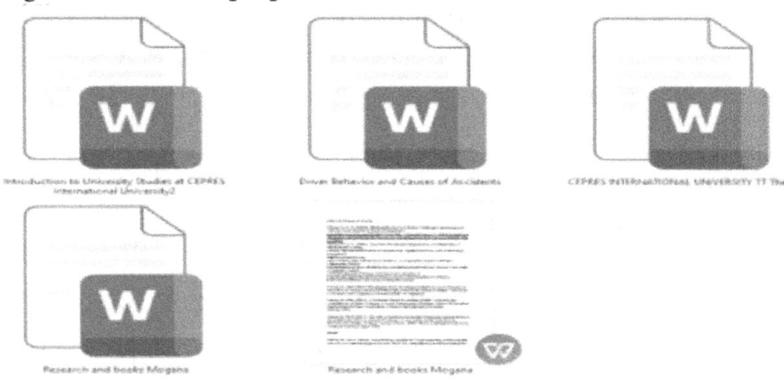

Figure 16: showing files with distinct names and purposes

Folders (Directories):

To bring order and structure to the multitude of files, operating systems introduce folders or directories. Folders act as virtual containers, providing a means to organize and group related files together. This hierarchical arrangement allows users to create a logical structure for their digital assets.

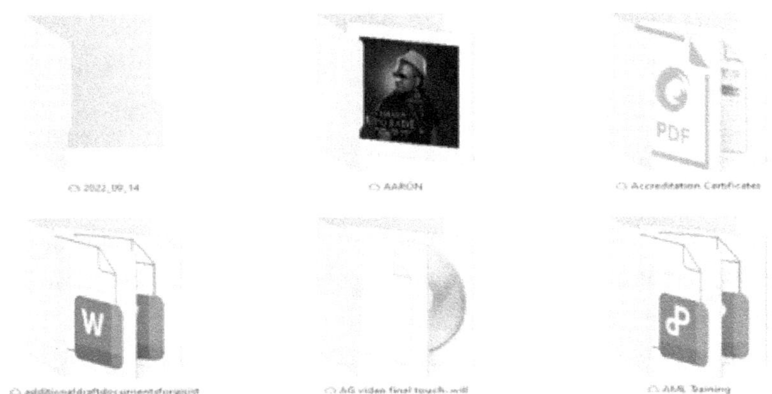

Figure 17: Folders with each of them containing as many files as possible

7.2.1.3 Drives or Volumes:

OPERATING SYSTEMS INTERACT with physical or virtual storage units known as drives or volumes. Drives can house multiple folders and files, serving as the overarching repositories for digital data. These storage units can be local drives within a computer or external volumes, and their capacity varies based on the storage medium.

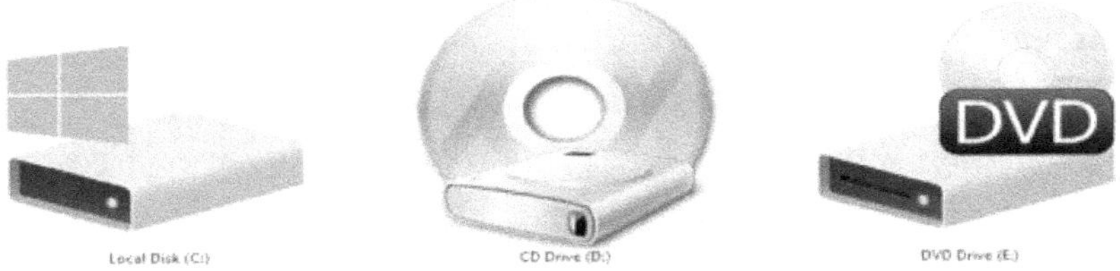

Figure 18: Drives that house multiple folders and files

IN ESSENCE, THE HIERARCHY of data organization, moving from individual files to folders and encompassing entire drives, forms the backbone of efficient file management. This structured approach not only simplifies the process of navigating through digital content but also enhances the overall accessibility and utility of the operating system for its users.

7.2.2 File Operations:

IN OPERATING SYSTEMS, users engage in a harmonious dance of creating, organizing, and manipulating files and folders. Let's delve into the key maneuvers of this digital symphony:

7.2.2.1 Creating Files and Folders:

FILES: These are the digital embodiments of documents, images, scripts, and an array of data. Users craft files to encapsulate and store specific information or content types.

Folders: Acting as the conductors of organization, folders are virtual directories that categorize and house files. Users employ folders to create structured repositories, making it easier to manage and locate related files.

7.2.2.2 Renaming and Deleting:

RENAMING: Users wield the power to assign files and folders new, descriptive names. This ensures that digital entities are easily recognizable and align with their contents.

Deleting: When files or folders outlive their utility, users have the option to permanently remove them. Deleting marks the end of a digital entity's existence within a system.

7.2.2.3 Copying and Moving:

COPYING: Duplicating files or folders is a fundamental maneuver, allowing users to create backups or replicate content. This function safeguards against data loss and facilitates easy sharing.

Moving: Transferring files or folders to different locations within the system aids in the ongoing organization. Whether reorganizing content or optimizing storage, moving is a pivotal file management action.

7.2.2.4 Sorting and Searching:

SORTING: Operating systems provide users with the ability to arrange files based on specific criteria. Sorting can be done alphabetically, chronologically, or by size, offering tailored views for efficient navigation.

Searching: In the vast expanse of digital content, users can employ search functionality to pinpoint specific files. This accelerates the retrieval process, especially in systems housing extensive data.

In this digital symphony of file management, users orchestrate the creation, renaming, deletion, copying, moving, sorting, and searching of files and folders. These maneuvers, akin to musical notes, contribute to the harmonious arrangement and accessibility of digital content within the operating system.

7.2.3 File Attributes and Permissions:

IN FILE MANAGEMENT, the concept of file attributes and permissions acts as the guardian of digital assets. Let's unravel the components that govern access and actions within this digital terrain:

7.2.3.1 File Attributes:

READ: Comparable to peering into the contents of a file, the 'Read' attribute allows users to view the information encapsulated within.

Write: Empowering users to modify or append content, the 'Write' attribute facilitates the dynamic evolution of files.

Execute: Reserved for executable files, the 'Execute' attribute bestows the ability to run these files, executing specific actions or programs.

7.2.3.2 Permissions:

OWNER, GROUP, AND OTHERS: The triumvirate of ownership delineates permissions for different entities. The owner, the group to which the file belongs, and others outside this realm have distinct permissions regarding reading, writing, and executing.

Access Control Lists (ACLs): Elevating control to a granular level, ACLs furnish detailed management of file access. This includes specifying permissions for specific users, tailoring access based on individual requirements.

In essence, file attributes and permissions serve as the custodians of the digital kingdom. They define who can interact with files, what actions are permissible, and the extent to which each digital denizen can contribute or consume. This meticulous control ensures the security, integrity, and tailored management of files within the operating system.

7.2.4 Practical Tips for Efficient File Management:

IN THE INTRICATE TAPESTRY of digital landscapes, mastering the art of file management is akin to orchestrating a symphony. Here are practical tips that serve as the notes to a harmonious and organized digital composition:

7.2.4.1 Use Descriptive Filenames:

CLARITY IN NAMING: Opt for filenames that are not just labels but concise descriptors of the file's contents. A well-chosen name swiftly unveils the essence of the digital manuscript.

7.2.4.2 Organize Files in Folders:

CATEGORIZATION BRILLIANCE: Harness the power of folders to weave a narrative of order. Sort files into folders based on projects, subjects, or thematic threads. This organizational ballet ensures swift retrieval and systematic storage.

7.2.4.3 Regularly Backup Important Files:

GUARDIANSHIP OF DATA: Fortify your data's resilience by embracing the habit of regular backups. Shielding important files from the whims of unforeseen events becomes a digital imperative.

7.2.4.4 Empty Recycle Bin or Trash:

SPACE RECLAMATION: Periodically sweep away the remnants of digital ephemera. Empty the recycle bin or trash to liberate storage space, ensuring a nimble and efficient digital ecosystem.

Incorporating these practical tips into your digital routine transforms the chaos of data into a sonnet of order. Just as a well-organized library invites exploration, an efficiently managed digital space beckons you to navigate with ease and purpose.

7.2.5 Overview of File Systems:

FILE SYSTEMS SERVE as the mapmakers, guiding our journey through the labyrinth of data. Here's a glimpse into three prominent cartographers: FAT32, NTFS, and exFAT.

7.2.5.1 FAT32 (File Allocation Table 32):

THE PIONEER: FAT32 stands as a testament to compatibility. With its roots tracing back to the early days, this file system holds the virtue of universality, seamlessly traversing various operating systems.

7.2.5.2 NTFS (New Technology File System):

THE MODERN MAESTRO: NTFS emerges as a sophisticated virtuoso, introducing new dimensions to file management. With advanced features and a robust security apparatus, it offers a contemporary symphony of efficiency and protection for your digital assets.

7.2.5.3 exFAT (Extended File Allocation Table):

THE TRAVELER'S COMPANION: exFAT becomes the perfect companion for external journeys. Specifically crafted for flash drives and external storage, it provides the flexibility and portability needed for the modern explorer.

The choice of file system becomes the choreography that defines the rhythm of access, security, and adaptability. Whether clinging to the nostalgic tunes of FAT32, embracing the avant-garde arrangements of NTFS, or opting for the nimble steps of exFAT, each system contributes to the symphony of our digital experiences.

Effective file management is a fundamental skill that enhances productivity and organization in the digital realm. As you progress through this course, you will delve deeper into specific file management systems and applications. CIU envisions that this knowledge will empower you to manage digital information efficiently, contributing to your academic and professional success. Let's continue this learning journey together!

8 Introduction to Productivity Software

8.1 Word Processing

WELCOME TO THE MODULE on "Word Processing" at CEPRES International University. In this session, we will explore the fundamental concepts of word processing, a crucial skill for academic and professional communication. CIU recognizes the significance of proficient word processing skills and aims to equip you with the knowledge needed for effective document creation.

8.1.1 Understanding Word Processing:

IN DIGITAL CREATION, word processing emerges as the maestro, orchestrating the harmonious composition of text documents. Let's unravel the intricacies of this versatile tool and explore its key features.

Definition and Purpose: Word processing is the artistic endeavor of creating, refining, and stylizing text documents through specialized software. This digital canvas serves a myriad of purposes, from scholarly papers to meticulous reports and the finesse of professional correspondence.

8.1.1.1 Key Features of Word Processing Software:

TEXT EDITING: The virtuosity of word processing lies in its ability to manipulate text seamlessly. Users can add, delete, or modify text with the grace of a skilled artisan.

Formatting: Elevating the aesthetics, formatting allows the adjustment of font styles, sizes, and alignments. It's the sartorial touch that defines the visual allure of the document.

Page Layout: Just as a canvas needs a frame, word processing sets the stage by defining margins, page orientation, and spacing. The layout becomes the backdrop for the textual performance.

Inserting Elements: Going beyond the realms of mere text, word processing introduces a visual symphony. Images, tables, and other elements find their place, enriching the narrative tapestry.

In digital literature, word processing transcends mere functionality; it becomes a dynamic medium where creativity meets functionality. It's the virtuoso's instrument, empowering users to weave words into eloquent compositions, each document a testament to the synergy of technology and expression.

8.1.2

Figure 19:(*Microsoft Word Images Free - Google Search, n.d.*)

Introduction to Microsoft Word:

IN WORD PROCESSING, Microsoft Word stands as the harbinger of textual creation and refinement. Let's embark on an exploration of its interface and delve into the artistry of document creation and formatting.

8.1.2.1 Interface Overview:

RIBBON: A virtual palette adorned with various tabs, each housing a symphony of related commands. It's the orchestrator of the creative ensemble.

Document Area: The expansive canvas where the narrative unfolds. Here, creators wield their digital quills, giving life to ideas and concepts.

Status Bar: A humble informant, residing at the document's feet, providing insights into the manuscript's vital statistics.

8.1.2.2 Document Creation and Editing:

TYPING AND DELETING *Text*: The foundational keystrokes, where each key depression births a letter, a word, a story. Deleting, the silent editor erasing the narrative's imperfections.

Copy, Cut, and Paste: The duplication, relocation, and transference. Text pirouettes across the digital stage, finding its rightful place.

Formatting Text:

Font Styles: Text, not confined to mere letters; it metamorphoses with font styles, a visual representation of the author's tone and expression.

Paragraph Formatting: Spacing, indentation, and alignment – the choreography of the written dance. Each paragraph finds its rhythm, its place on the page.

Bullets and Numbering: Lists, the curated catalog of ideas. Bullets and numbers, the curators, arranging concepts in harmony.

As we navigate the interface and wield the tools, Microsoft Word transforms into the author's accomplice, breathing life into ideas. It's not merely a software; it's a medium where creativity and functionality dance hand in hand, producing symphonies of words that resonate with the soul.

8.1.3 Document Layout and Design:

IN THE INTRICATE TAPESTRY of document creation, Microsoft Word unfolds as a loom, weaving together elements of page layout and design. Let's embark on a journey through the dimensions of pages and the artistic infusion of images and shapes.

8.1.3.1 Page Layout:

MARGINS AND ORIENTATION: Here, the page transforms from a blank canvas to a structured stage. Margins delineate the boundaries, while orientation sets the stage – portrait or landscape, the choice shapes the narrative.

Headers and Footers: The crowning and grounding embellishments of each page. Headers whisper essential details at the page's zenith, while footers offer a firm foundation at its nadir.

Page Numbers: A sequential manifesto etched at the bottom, guiding the reader through the document's chronicles.

8.1.3.2 Inserting Elements:

IMAGES AND SHAPES: The artistic strokes on the canvas. Images, the visual anecdotes, and shapes, the geometric musings, add layers to the narrative, transcending words.

Tables: A tabular design, where information aligns into organized formations. Cells and rows, the meticulous architects of structured data.

Hyperlinks: Hyperlinks transcend the document, connecting to the vast landscapes of digital knowledge.

As the loom of Microsoft Word deftly intertwines these elements, the document becomes a visual symphony, not just an arrangement of words but a masterpiece of layout and design. It's a testament to the fusion of creativity and functionality, where the author's vision materializes into a visual narrative that captivates and informs.

8.1.4 Document Review and Collaboration:

IN THE VAST EXPANSE of document creation, the journey doesn't end with composition. Microsoft Word extends its provisions to ensure the document's integrity through meticulous review and collaboration features.

8.1.4.1 Spell Check and Grammar:

SPELL CHECK: Scanning the text for errant spells, ensuring that every word stands correct and true.

Grammar Check: The grammatical custodian, examining the structure of sentences, ensuring linguistic harmony.

8.1.4.2 Collaborative Editing:

TRACK CHANGES: A collaborative work into the document's fabric. Each edit, a footprint in the evolution of the document. Authors' contributions are recorded visually.

Comments: The silent conversations within the document's margins. Comments are the discourse – questions, clarifications, and insights shared amongst collaborators. A virtual dialogue that transcends the boundaries of space and time.

As the document undergoes this meticulous scrutiny, it transforms into a refined artifact, polished by the collective intellect of its authors. Microsoft Word, the scribe's ally, not only aids in the initial creation but also ensures the document's fluency, correctness, and coherence in the collaborative voyage of ideas and words.

8.1.5 Practical Tips for Effective Word Processing:

EMBARKING ON THE SEAS of word processing requires not just skill but also a compass to navigate the challenges. Microsoft Word, a sailor's trusted companion, offers practical tips for a smooth voyage.

8.1.5.1 Use Styles for Consistency:

FORMATTING: Harmonize your document's appearance using predefined styles. Consistency becomes the melody that resonates through each paragraph and page.

Effortless Elegance: Let your headers, subheadings, and body text be in uniformity. Styles grant you the power to orchestrate a document that is both visually appealing and structurally sound.

8.1.5.2 Save and Backup Regularly:

ARCHIVE: Create a lifeboat for your document through regular saving. In unexpected events, an up-to-date archive ensures your work stays available.

Guardian Backups: Sail with confidence, knowing that backup copies stand as guardians against the storms of technological mishaps.

8.1.5.3 Utilize Templates for Efficiency:

TEMPLATES: Begin your journey with a navigational guide – document templates. These templates act as your compass, providing direction and expediting the creation process.

Efficiency Anchored: Why start from scratch when templates can anchor your document creation? Do your work efficiently with templates tailored to your needs.

Microsoft Word equips you with these practical tips. As you chart your course through the document these insights ensure a work done with ease, consistency, and efficiency.

8.1.6 Overview of Other Word Processing Software:

VENTURING INTO THE expansive world of word processing extends beyond Microsoft Word. Discover new places with Google Docs and LibreOffice Writer, each offering unique landscapes for your document journeys.

8.1.6.1 Google Docs:

CLOUD-CRAFTED COLLABORATION: Sail into the collaborative clouds with Google Docs, where multiple individuals can contribute to the same document simultaneously.

Accessible Anywhere: Dock your document in the cloud, accessible from any port. Google Docs ensures your work is not tethered to a single vessel but travels freely across the digital space.

8.1.6.2 LibreOffice Writer:

OPEN-SOURCE OASIS: Explore open-source wonders with LibreOffice Writer. An open sea of features awaits, where freedom and flexibility reign.

All-Inclusive Archipelago: The archipelago of features – from advanced formatting to document templates – invites you to traverse the vastness of document creation.

As you set sail into these uncharted territories, may Google Docs and LibreOffice Writer be your trusted companions, offering diverse experiences and adding new dimensions to your word processing expeditions.

Proficient word processing skills are essential for academic and professional success. As you progress through this course, you will explore advanced features and applications of word processing software. CIU envisions that this knowledge will empower you to communicate effectively through written documents, contributing to your growth as a student and future professional. Let's continue this learning journey together!

8.2 Spreadsheet Software

WELCOME TO THE MODULE on "Spreadsheet Software" at CEPRES International University. In this session, we will delve into the essential concepts of spreadsheet usage, a crucial skill for data analysis, organization, and management. CIU recognizes the significance of spreadsheet skills and aims to equip you with the knowledge needed for effective data manipulation and presentation.

8.2.1 Understanding Spreadsheet Software:

JOURNEY INTO THE LAND of numbers and data with spreadsheet software, a vessel designed for the seamless organization, analysis, and presentation of your numerical tales.

8.2.1.1 Basic Components:

CELLS AND GRID: Navigate the sea of cells, each a unique coordinate in the vast grid. These cells form the foundation where your data finds its place.

Formulas and Functions: Unleash the power of mathematical magic with formulas and functions. Watch as your spreadsheet transforms, performing intricate calculations at your command.

Charts and Graphs: Cast your data into the visual realm with charts and graphs. Illuminate your narratives and unveil insights that transcend the boundaries of mere numbers.

8.2.1.2 Versatility:

DATA ORGANIZATION: Steer through the waves of data, organizing and structuring your information with the precision of a seasoned professional.

Calculation Capabilities: Harness calculation with formulas that breathe life into your data. From simple arithmetic to complex computations, your spreadsheet is a versatile calculator.

8.2.1.3 Decision-Making Expedition:

ANALYSIS: Embark on an analysis expedition, where trends and patterns emerge from the depths of your data, guiding you toward informed decision-making.

Presentation Excellence: Hoist the sails of presentation excellence as your data transforms into visually stunning charts and graphs, ready to captivate any audience.

As you embark on your odyssey with spreadsheet software, may your numbers be ever organized, calculations precise, and data-driven decisions as clear as the azure sea. May your journey be filled with insights, and your spreadsheets be a testament to the art of navigating the numerical seas.

8.2.2 Introduction to Microsoft Excel:

EMBARK ON A VOYAGE into the data-driven territories with Microsoft Excel, a mighty vessel equipped to cultivate numbers and charts.

Figure 20: Icon for Microsoft Excel

8.2.2.1 Navigational Instruments:

WORKBOOK AND WORKSHEETS: Behold the workbook, a volume that houses worksheets, the canvases for your numerical epics.

Columns and Rows: Navigate the vast sea of cells organized into columns and rows, creating a structured tableau for your data to thrive.

Cell Referencing: Unleash the power of cell referencing, a compass guiding you to specific locations within the spreadsheet.

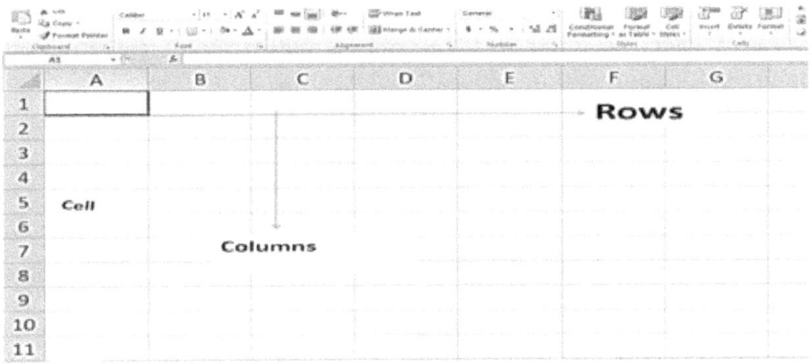

Figure 21 A spread sheet showing row, columns, and cells

8.2.2.2 Data Pioneering:

ENTERING DATA: Chart your course by inputting data – values, text, and dates – into the cells, crafting the narrative of your numerical narrative.

Cell Formatting: Customize your work with cell formatting. Adjust fonts, colors, and number formats to bring your data to life.

Data Validation: Ensure the integrity of your narrative with data validation rules, safeguarding against inaccuracies.

8.2.2.3 Charting Your Course:

FORMULAS AND FUNCTIONS: Set sail into the world of formulas and functions, where calculations become the wind in your spreadsheet.

Charts and Graphs: Transform your data into visual masterpieces with charts and graphs, allowing your audience to navigate the narrative with ease.

Excel Excellence: As you navigate Excel, may your workbooks be well-organized, your formulas ever precise, and your charts a beacon of clarity in the numerical expanse. May your data-driven journey through Microsoft Excel be filled with discoveries and insights, turning your numerical odyssey into an unparalleled adventure.

8.2.3 Formulas and Functions:

EMBARK ON A FORMULAIC odyssey within the sacred halls of Microsoft Excel, where the arcane arts of calculations and functions weave the tapestry of data manipulation.

8.2.3.1 Navigating the Basic Waters:

SUM, AVERAGE, COUNT: Navigate the foundational seas with these stalwart companions. Sum tallies the treasures, Average finds the middle ground, and Count enumerates the crew.

Concatenate: Unite disparate text fragments into a harmonious whole, forging a cohesive narrative from scattered tales.

8.2.3.2 Venturing into Function-Filled Realms:

VLOOKUP AND HLOOKUP: Set sail on the lookup seas, where VLOOKUP searches vertically and HLOOKUP scans horizontally through vast tables to uncover hidden truths.

IF Statements: Navigate the straits of logic, where IF Statements become the compass of decision-making. Sail through conditions, choosing routes based on the winds of true or false.

Excel's Formulaic Legacy: In the fabled halls of Excel, formulas are the spells that summon numerical enchantments. As you traverse these seas, may your formulas be error-free, your functions ever precise, and your data transformations legendary. May your odyssey through the formulaic realms of Microsoft Excel be marked by revelations and insights, turning your spreadsheet into an enchanted grimoire of calculations.

8.2.4 Data Analysis and Visualization:

EMBARK ON A JOURNEY through Microsoft Excel, where data analysis and visualization weave insight and understanding.

8.2.4.1 Charting the Course with Visual Elegance:

BAR, LINE, PIE CHARTS: Conjure visual masterpieces to represent your data. Let the Bars rise, Lines weave tales, and Pies slice through complexity, transforming raw numbers into visual poetry.

Sparklines: Infuse magic into individual cells with Sparklines – tiny, dynamic charts that whisper volumes of insight within a confined space.

8.2.4.2 PivotTables: The Arcane Altar of Data Sorcery:

DATA SUMMARIZATION: Enter PivotTables, where vast datasets bow to your command. Summarize data effortlessly, wielding the power to distill complexity into simplicity.

Dynamic Filtering: Peer into the crystal ball of dynamic filtering. Witness the fluid transformation of perspectives, revealing new views of understanding as you filter through the blankets of data.

Crafting Data into Visual Spells: In Microsoft Excel, charts and PivotTables are your wands, transforming dull numbers into captivating visual spells. May your charts be compelling, your Sparklines shine bright, and your PivotTables reveal the arcane patterns hidden in your data. As you journey through these realms, may your insights be profound and your visualizations, legendary.

8.2.5 Data Management and Collaboration:

8.2.5.1 Sorting Data:

IN THE DATA EXPANSE, where chaos may reign, sorting emerges as the compass to navigate these uncharted challenges. Ascendancy of alphabetical order, numerical precision, or chronological majesty—all at your fingertips. As you click, watch the rows realign, forming a disciplined fleet of information. Sorting is not just organization; it's the art of unveiling patterns and unraveling insights.

8.2.5.2 Filtering Data:

UNVEILING HIDDEN ISLES of Insight Behold the power to filter—a treasure map revealing hidden isles of information within your dataset. Click and watch as the irrelevant recedes, leaving only the gems you seek. Filter by value, by condition, or create custom passages through the data archipelago. Filtering is the lantern that illuminates the path to profound revelations.

8.2.5.3 Collaborative Editing:

THE SHARED VOYAGE IN this collaborative odyssey, comments and track changes are your messages in a bottle, tossed into the digital sea. Communicate with fellow navigators, record the winds of alterations, and leave your mark on the shores of shared knowledge. Sharing and permissions are the seals on the scrolls, ensuring secure collaboration—granting access to some, restricting to others.

As you embark on this data odyssey, may your sorts be swift, your filters precise, and your collaborations, a harmonious symphony of insights. Navigate the seas of data with confidence, for in Microsoft Excel, you are the captain of your analytical destiny.

8.2.6 Practical Tips for Effective Spreadsheet Use:

EMBARK ON A JOURNEY to master the intricacies of Microsoft Excel with these practical tips, transforming your spreadsheet voyage into a seamless and efficient expedition.

8.2.6.1 Use Named Ranges:

IN THE VAST OCEAN OF cells, named ranges are your navigational inspirations. Assign meaningful names to cell ranges, transforming numerical coordinates into descriptive signposts. Easily reference these inspirations in formulas and charts, ensuring clarity in your data navigation.

8.2.6.2 Document Versioning:

AS YOU SAIL THROUGH the epochs of data, let versioning be your time-travel companion. Create different versions of your spreadsheet, capturing the essence of each moment. Safeguard against the perils of unintended changes and navigate through the currents of data evolution with confidence.

8.2.6.3 Protect Important Formulas:

WITHIN THE FORTRESS of your spreadsheet, critical formulas stand as guardians of insight. Fortify their sanctity by locking cells or entire sheets. This shield prevents accidental alterations, ensuring the integrity of your calculations. Let not the waves of inadvertent changes breach the walls of your analytical stronghold.

Embark on your Excel expedition armed with these tips, and may your journey through cells and columns be a triumphant saga of efficiency and precision. May your formulas remain inviolate, your ranges named with purpose, and your versions tell the tales of your data conquests. Onward, intrepid navigator, to excel in the seas of spreadsheets!

8.2.6.4 Overview of Other Spreadsheet Software:

GOOGLE SHEETS: Navigating the Cloud for Collaborative Charting Explore cloud-based spreadsheet collaboration with Google Sheets. As your data takes flight in the virtual sky, multiple hands can steer the ship simultaneously. Experience real-time collaboration and seamless sharing, allowing your data to chart new courses in the boundless skies of the cloud.

LibreOffice Calc: With LibreOffice Calc, a versatile spreadsheet software offering an array of features. As you navigate through the currents of data manipulation, experience the freedom of customization and the openness of collaborative exploration. Join the community-driven journey into the expansive sea of open-source spreadsheet solutions.

Proficient spreadsheet skills are essential for data-driven decision-making and organizational efficiency. As you progress through this course, you will explore advanced features and applications of spreadsheet software. CIU envisions that this knowledge will empower you to handle and analyze data effectively, contributing to your success in academia and beyond. Let's continue this learning journey together!

8.3 Presentation Software

WELCOME TO THE MODULE on "Presentation Software" at CEPRES International University. In this session, we will explore the fundamental concepts of presentation creation, a crucial skill for academic, professional, and public communication. CIU recognizes the significance of presentation skills and aims to equip you with the knowledge needed for effective visual storytelling.

8.3.1 Understanding Presentation Software:

EMBARK ON A JOURNEY into presentation software, where words, images, and multimedia elements converge to weave compelling visual narratives. In this digital theater of ideas, key features such as slides, text boxes, and dynamic transitions take center stage. The purpose is clear: to captivate, inform, and leave a lasting impression on the audience. Welcome to the world of visual storytelling, where each slide is a canvas for creativity, and every presentation is a performance.

8.3.2 Introduction to Microsoft PowerPoint:

Figure 22: Microsoft PowerPoint Icon

IN DIGITAL CREATIVITY, Microsoft PowerPoint stands as a versatile canvas, allowing users to bring their ideas to life in a visually compelling manner. The interface is akin to a storyboard, offering a comprehensive set of tools and features to weave a captivating narrative.

The Slides Pane, a panoramic overview of the entire presentation, serves as the starting point. Here, presenters can strategically plan the flow of their content, ensuring a seamless and logical progression. It's the director's view, providing a bird's-eye perspective to organize thoughts and concepts.

The Ribbon and Tabs emerge as the artists' palette, offering an extensive array of creative tools. These tools empower presenters to add layers of depth to their presentations. Whether it's incorporating images, shaping text, or enhancing the visual appeal with various features, the Ribbon and Tabs provide the means to sculpt each slide into a visual masterpiece.

Behind the scenes, the Notes Pane acts as a backstage pass for the presenter. It offers a space to jot down additional insights, cues, or reminders. This feature allows for a more dynamic and engaging presentation, where the audience experiences not just what's on the surface but also benefits from the presenter's depth of knowledge.

Creating and editing slides becomes an art form with PowerPoint. The ability to insert slides seamlessly ensures that the storyline unfolds cohesively. Text and bullet points serve as the building blocks, allowing presenters to structure content effectively, delivering information in a clear and organized manner.

The formatting options within PowerPoint provide a spectrum of choices to refine the visual aesthetics. Font styles, color schemes, and background designs offer a level of customization that goes beyond mere information delivery. Each slide becomes a carefully curated visual experience, enhancing audience engagement.

In essence, Microsoft PowerPoint transcends the traditional notion of presentations. It transforms information sharing into a dynamic and interactive storytelling experience. The presenter becomes the director of a visual symphony, orchestrating ideas and concepts with precision, leaving a lasting impact on the audience.

8.3.3 Enhancing Presentations:

EMBARKING ON THE JOURNEY of enhancing presentations, Microsoft PowerPoint offers a plethora of features that transcend the boundaries of traditional slideshows. The canvas becomes dynamic, with multimedia elements and animations elevating presentations to captivating experiences.

Multimedia Elements:

Inserting Images and Graphics: The visual appeal of a presentation is significantly amplified by the strategic use of images and graphics.

PowerPoint allows presenters to seamlessly insert visuals, ranging from photographs to illustrations. This feature not only adds aesthetic value but also serves as a powerful tool for conveying complex ideas in a digestible format.

8.3.3.1 Embedding Videos and Audio:

ELEVATING ENGAGEMENT to new heights, the option to embed videos and audio brings a multimedia dimension to presentations. Whether it's showcasing a product in action or incorporating a relevant audio snippet, this feature provides a dynamic and immersive experience for the audience.

8.3.3.2 Transitions and Animations:

SLIDE TRANSITIONS:
Transitioning from one slide to the next is not merely a shift but an artful progression. PowerPoint provides an array of slide transition options, allowing presenters to choose the style that best complements their narrative. From subtle fades to dynamic slides, each transition sets the stage for what follows, creating a seamless and visually appealing journey.

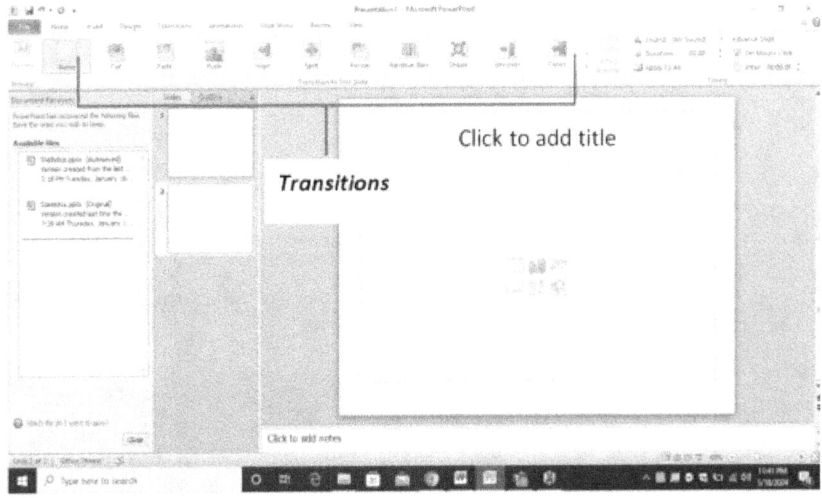

Figure 23: Powerpoint showing location of transitions

Object Animations:

Beyond static content, PowerPoint empowers presenters to breathe life into their slides through object animations. Elements on a slide can be animated to appear, disappear, or move across the screen, adding a layer of dynamism to the presentation. This feature isn't just about visual aesthetics; it's a storytelling tool that enables presenters to emphasize key points, guide the audience's focus, and maintain engagement.

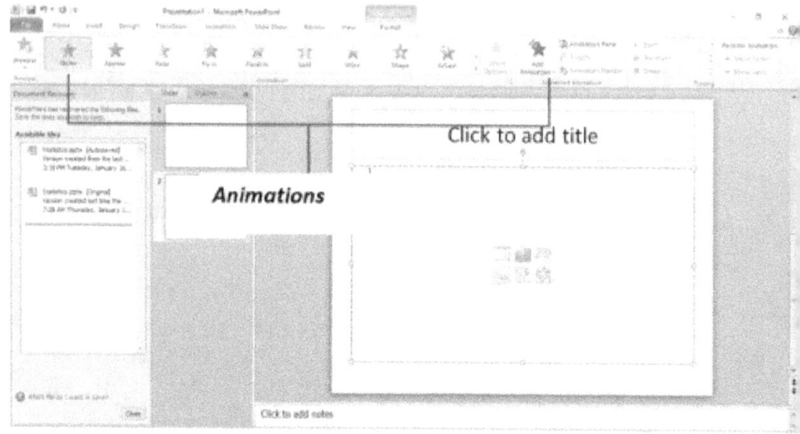

Figure 24: PowerPoint showing Animations

In enhancing presentations, these multimedia elements and animations transcend the conventional boundaries of static slides. PowerPoint becomes a canvas where information isn't just delivered; it's experienced. Each slide becomes a stage where visuals, audio, and animations collaborate to convey a narrative that resonates with the audience, making the presentation an unforgettable journey.

8.3.4 Tips for Effective Presentations:

CLEAR AND CONCISE CONTENT:

Effectiveness in presentations begins with clarity and conciseness. Emphasizing key points while avoiding information overload ensures that the audience can grasp and retain the core message. By distilling complex ideas into digestible nuggets, presenters create a framework that resonates with the audience.

Engaging Visuals:

Visual elements are potent tools for maintaining audience interest and enhancing comprehension. Incorporating visuals, such as images, graphics, and charts, complements spoken content. Well-designed visuals not only reinforce key messages but also provide a dynamic and memorable dimension to the presentation.

Practice and Timing:

A well-rehearsed presentation is a key to success. Practice allows presenters to fine-tune their delivery, ensuring a smooth and confident performance. Being mindful of timing is equally crucial; a well-paced presentation respects the audience's time and keeps them engaged. Rehearsing also helps presenters anticipate potential challenges and be prepared to handle them effectively.

In summary, effective presentations are founded on the principles of clarity, engagement, and preparation. Clear and concise content forms the backbone, engaging visuals captivate the audience, and diligent practice ensures a polished and well-timed delivery. These tips serve as guiding principles for presenters striving to make a lasting impact and deliver presentations that resonate with their audience.

8.3.5 Collaborative Presentation:

COLLABORATIVE EDITING:

Collaboration is a cornerstone of modern work environments, and collaborative presentation tools facilitate seamless teamwork. Within platforms like Microsoft PowerPoint, users can collaborate with others on a presentation in real-time. This collaborative editing feature allows multiple contributors to work on the same set of slides simultaneously, fostering synergy among team members.

Sharing and Reviewing Slides:

Collaborative presentation tools enable users to share their slides with others effortlessly. This sharing capability allows team members, stakeholders, or clients to review and provide feedback on the presentation content. Comments and suggestions can be exchanged directly within the presentation interface, streamlining the feedback loop and enhancing communication.

Version History:

Version history is a valuable feature that keeps track of changes made to the presentation over time. This functionality allows users to revisit earlier versions of the presentation, compare changes, and even revert to a previous state if necessary. Version history is particularly useful in collaborative settings, providing transparency and accountability for all edits made by different contributors.

In conclusion, collaborative presentation tools empower teams to work together efficiently, ensuring that everyone involved can contribute, review, and track changes seamlessly. These features enhance teamwork, improve communication, and ultimately result in more polished and well-rounded presentations.

8.3.6 Practical Tips for Presentation Software Use:

CONSISTENT DESIGN:

Consistency in design is a fundamental aspect of creating visually appealing and professional presentations. It involves using a uniform theme, font style, color scheme, and layout throughout the entire presentation. By maintaining a consistent design, the audience experiences a cohesive and polished visual narrative, making it easier to follow and understand the content.

Audience Interaction:

Enhancing audience engagement is crucial for delivering impactful presentations. Presentation software often offers features that enable audience interaction. For example, incorporating interactive elements like polls or Q&A sessions can captivate the audience's attention and make the presentation more dynamic. This not only keeps the audience involved but also provides opportunities for real-time feedback and participation.

By implementing these practical tips, presenters can elevate the quality of their presentations, making them more visually appealing, coherent, and engaging for the audience.

8.3.7 Overview of Other Presentation Software:

Figure 25:(Google Slides Images - Google Search, n.d.)

GOOGLE SLIDES: Google Slides is a cloud-based presentation software that allows users to create, edit, and collaborate on presentations online. It is part of the Google Workspace suite and provides seamless integration with other Google apps. With real-time collaboration features, users can work together on presentations, making it an excellent choice for teams or individuals who prefer cloud-based solutions.

LibreOffice Impress: LibreOffice Impress is an open-source alternative for creating presentations. It is part of the LibreOffice suite, offering a range of features for designing and delivering slideshows. LibreOffice Impress supports various multimedia elements, transitions, and animations, making it a versatile option for users who seek free and open-source software alternatives for presentation creation.

Proficient presentation skills are essential for effective communication in various settings. As you progress through this course, you will explore advanced features and applications of presentation software. CIU envisions that this knowledge will empower you to deliver impactful presentations, contributing to your success as a student and future professional. Let's continue this learning journey together!

9 Internet Skills for Academic Success & Email Communication

9.1 Navigating Online Resources

WELCOME TO THE MODULE on "Navigating Online Resources" at CEPRES International University. In this session, we will explore essential skills for effectively navigating the vast world of online information. CIU, recognizes the importance of online research and aims to equip you with the knowledge needed for efficient and accurate exploration of digital resources.

9.1.1 Introduction to Online Navigation:

IN THE CONTEMPORARY digital age, the ability to navigate online resources effectively is paramount for academic research and learning. Online resources encompass a vast array of information available on the internet, ranging from websites and databases to digital libraries. Navigating these resources is an essential skill for individuals engaged in academic pursuits.

9.1.1.1 Understanding Online Resources:

- *Websites:* These are web-based platforms that can host a variety of content, including articles, blogs, reports, and more. Websites can be created by individuals, organizations, or institutions and serve as valuable sources of information.
- **Databases:** Databases are organized collections of data that can be searched, retrieved, and manipulated. In an academic context, databases often contain scholarly articles, research papers, and other resources relevant to specific fields of study.
- *Digital Libraries:* Digital libraries house digitized versions

of books, journals, manuscripts, and other written materials. They provide a convenient way for users to access a wealth of information without the need for physical copies.

9.1.1.2 Importance of Online Navigation:

- ***Enhanced Research Productivity:*** Efficient online navigation contributes significantly to research productivity. With the vast amount of information available online, the ability to quickly locate relevant sources saves time and allows researchers to focus on the substance of their work.
- ***Critical Evaluation Skills:*** Navigating online resources involves not just finding information but also critically evaluating its reliability, credibility, and relevance. Students and researchers need to develop discerning skills to sift through the abundance of online data and identify trustworthy sources.
- ***Access to Current Information***: Online navigation ensures access to the most current and up-to-date information. Unlike traditional printed materials, online resources can be updated in real-time, providing users with the latest developments in their respective fields.
- **Global Accessibility:** Online resources offer global accessibility, enabling individuals to access information from anywhere with an internet connection. This global reach facilitates collaboration, knowledge sharing, and a broader perspective on various subjects.

IN CONCLUSION, THE introduction to online navigation underscores its importance in the academic landscape. As the digital realm continues to evolve, the ability to navigate online resources adeptly becomes an indispensable skill for students, researchers, and anyone engaged in the pursuit of knowledge.

9.1.2 Efficient Internet Browsing:

NAVIGATING THE VAST landscape of the internet efficiently requires specific techniques and skills. Whether conducting research, gathering information, or simply exploring, individuals can enhance their internet browsing experience through the following strategies:

9.1.2.1 Browsing Techniques:

- ***Search Engine Basics***: The foundation of efficient internet browsing lies in mastering search engine basics. Popular search engines like Google provide a user-friendly interface, but understanding how to formulate effective search queries is crucial. This involves using relevant keywords and being aware of search operators.
- ***Boolean Operators***: Refining search queries with Boolean operators such as AND, OR, and NOT allows users to customize their search results. This can help in narrowing down or broadening the scope of information based on specific requirements.
- ***Advanced Search Features***: Many search engines offer advanced features and filters that users can leverage for more targeted results. These may include date filters, site-specific searches, and file-type filters. Knowing how to use these features enhances precision in internet searches.

9.1.2.2 Evaluating Website Credibility:

- ***Source Authority***: Assessing the authority of the source is crucial for determining the credibility of the information.

Reliable sources often come from reputable institutions, experts in the field, or established organizations. Users should be wary of information from unknown or questionable sources.

- *Publication Date*: The recency of information is essential, especially in fields where knowledge evolves rapidly. Checking the publication date of an article or webpage ensures that the information is up-to-date and relevant to the current context.
- *Cross-Referencing Information*: To enhance the reliability of information, cross-referencing involves verifying facts or details from multiple sources. Consistency across different reputable sources strengthens the credibility of the information.

EFFICIENT INTERNET browsing is not just about finding information quickly but also about ensuring the accuracy and reliability of the content accessed. By mastering search engine techniques and adopting critical evaluation skills, users can navigate the internet with confidence, extracting valuable and trustworthy information for their needs.

9.1.3 Utilizing Online Databases:

ONLINE DATABASES PLAY a crucial role in academic research, providing access to a wealth of scholarly information. Efficiently navigating and utilizing these resources involves understanding different types of databases and employing effective search strategies:

9.1.3.1 Accessing Academic Databases:

LIBRARY DATABASES: Academic institutions often provide access to extensive databases that house scholarly articles, research papers, and publications. These databases cover a wide range of disciplines, and access is typically available to students and faculty.

Database Search Strategies: Crafting effective search queries is essential for retrieving relevant information from academic databases. Users should identify key terms, use Boolean operators, and consider advanced search features offered by the database platform to refine their search results.

9.1.3.2 Digital Libraries and Repositories:

OPEN ACCESS RESOURCES: Digital libraries with open access resources provide valuable content freely accessible to the public. These resources may include academic publications, books, and research materials. Examples include platforms like Project Gutenberg and OpenStax.

Archives and Repositories: Specialized archives and repositories focus on preserving and providing access to specific types of collections. These could include historical documents, cultural artifacts, or discipline-specific materials. Examples include institutional repositories of universities or digital archives of cultural institutions.

Efficient utilization of online databases involves familiarity with the specific databases relevant to one's field of study, as well as the development of effective search and retrieval skills. By leveraging library databases, employing targeted search strategies, and exploring open access resources, individuals can access a diverse array of scholarly materials to support their academic endeavors.

9.1.4 Citing Online Sources:

IN ACADEMIC WRITING, citing online sources is a fundamental practice that involves adhering to specific citation styles and adapting them to the unique characteristics of digital sources. This process ensures proper attribution, helps readers trace and verify information, and prevents plagiarism. The following details the components and considerations involved in citing online sources:

9.1.5 Understanding Citations:

CITATION STYLES: Common citation styles such as APA (American Psychological Association), MLA (Modern Language Association), and Chicago have distinct guidelines for citing various sources. These styles cover a range of materials, including books, articles, and online content. Each style prescribes specific formats for elements like author names, publication dates, titles, and page numbers.

Importance of Proper Citation: Proper citation serves multiple purposes. It acknowledges the original author's work, provides a trail for readers to explore cited sources, and upholds academic integrity by avoiding plagiarism. By following established citation styles, writers contribute to the scholarly conversation and maintain a standardized approach to referencing.

9.1.6 Digital Source Citations:

CITING WEBSITES AND Online Articles: When citing online sources, the essential components of a citation remain, but there are variations based on the citation style. For instance, in APA style, the inclusion of the URL is common, while in Chicago style, a publication description may be used. Writers need to adapt these styles to fit the digital context, considering factors like web page titles, publication dates, and website names.

DOI and URL Inclusion: Digital Object Identifiers (DOIs) are unique alphanumeric strings assigned to online publications. Including DOIs in citations, when available, enhances source identification and provides a stable link to the source. If a DOI is not present, providing the URL is crucial for directing readers to the online material. The URL should be accurate and accessible.

In the rapidly evolving digital landscape, where information is disseminated through online platforms, mastering the art of citing online sources is indispensable. Writers must be adept at navigating various citation styles and adapting them to the nuances of digital content, ensuring that their work reflects academic rigor and integrity.

9.1.7 Online Communication Etiquette:

EFFECTIVE ONLINE COMMUNICATION is essential for academic and professional interactions. Here are key aspects of online communication etiquette:

9.1.7.1 Professional Email Communication:

FORMAL EMAIL STRUCTURE: Crafting emails with a formal structure is crucial for academic and professional communication. This includes a clear and concise introduction, body, and conclusion. Maintaining a professional tone and avoiding casual language contributes to a respectful communication style.

Subject Line Importance: The subject line plays a vital role in email communication. It should provide a brief and accurate summary of the email's content. A well-crafted subject line enhances clarity and helps the recipient understand the email's purpose without opening it.

9.1.7.2 Collaborative Online Platforms:

EFFECTIVE USE OF ONLINE Platforms: Utilizing online platforms such as forums and discussion boards requires effective communication. Clearly expressing ideas, providing constructive feedback, and actively participating in discussions contribute to a collaborative and engaging online environment.

Netiquette: Observing proper online communication etiquette, often referred to as "netiquette," is essential. This includes being respectful, avoiding offensive language, and acknowledging others' contributions. Understanding the platform's guidelines and rules ensures a positive and professional online interaction.

9.1.7.3 General Tips for Online Communication:

CLEAR AND CONCISE COMMUNICATION:

- Clearly express ideas and thoughts to avoid misinterpretation.
- Be concise in your messages, keeping in mind the recipient's time.

Timely Responses:

- Respond to emails and messages in a timely manner to demonstrate professionalism and courtesy.

Use of Formal Language:

- Maintain a formal and professional language in written communication.

Privacy and Security:

- Be mindful of privacy and security concerns when sharing information online.

Acknowledgment of Receipt:

- Confirm receipt of important emails or messages, especially in professional settings.

Understanding Cultural Differences:

- Consider cultural differences in communication styles and adapt as needed, particularly in diverse online environments.

Avoiding All Caps and Emoticons:

- Refrain from using all capital letters or excessive emoticons in professional communication to maintain a polished appearance.

By adhering to these guidelines, individuals can contribute to a positive and respectful online communication environment, fostering effective collaboration and professionalism.

9.1.8 Cybersecurity Awareness:

CYBERSECURITY AWARENESS is crucial in the digital age to safeguard personal information and mitigate online threats. Here are key aspects of cybersecurity awareness:

9.1.8.1 Protecting Personal Information:

PASSWORD MANAGEMENT: Creating strong and secure passwords is fundamental to protecting personal information. Cybersecurity experts recommend using complex passwords that combine uppercase and lowercase letters, numbers, and symbols. Additionally, individuals should avoid using easily guessable information such as birthdays or common words. Employing unique passwords for different accounts enhances security, and regular password updates are advisable.

Avoiding Phishing Attempts: Phishing is a common online threat where attackers attempt to trick individuals into revealing sensitive information. Being aware of phishing attempts is crucial for cybersecurity. Common signs of phishing include unsolicited emails or messages requesting personal information, suspicious links, or messages designed to evoke urgency. Individuals should refrain from clicking on unfamiliar links and verify the legitimacy of communication, especially when it involves providing personal or financial information.

9.1.8.2 General Cybersecurity Practices:

USE OF TWO-FACTOR AUTHENTICATION (2FA):

- Enabling 2FA adds an extra layer of security, requiring users to provide additional verification beyond passwords.

Regular Software Updates:

- Keeping software, operating systems, and antivirus programs up to date ensures that security patches are applied, reducing vulnerabilities.

Secure Wi-Fi Connections:

- Using encrypted Wi-Fi connections with strong passwords prevents unauthorized access to personal networks.

Data Backups:

- Regularly backing up important data is essential to prevent data loss in the event of cybersecurity incidents.

Awareness of Social Engineering:

- Understanding social engineering tactics, where attackers manipulate individuals into divulging confidential information, is crucial for cybersecurity.

Firewall Protection:

- Activating firewalls provides an additional barrier against unauthorized access to devices and networks.

Safe Online Shopping and Banking:

- Ensuring secure connections (https://) when conducting online transactions and avoiding public Wi-Fi for sensitive activities enhances cybersecurity.

Educating Others:

- Sharing cybersecurity knowledge with friends, family, and colleagues contributes to a safer online community.

By adopting these cybersecurity practices, individuals can significantly reduce the risk of falling victim to online threats and contribute to creating a more secure digital environment. Ongoing education and awareness are key components of maintaining cybersecurity hygiene in an ever-evolving online landscape.

9.1.9 Practical Tips for Online Navigation:

9.1.9.1 Bookmarking and Organizing:

CREATING A SYSTEM FOR Bookmarking: One practical tip for effective online navigation is to develop a systematic approach to bookmarking. Users can organize their bookmarks by creating folders based on categories, topics, or projects. This helps in quickly accessing valuable online resources without having to rely on search engines every time. Most web browsers offer features for creating, organizing, and syncing bookmarks across devices, providing a seamless experience.

Organizing Valuable Online Resources: Beyond simple bookmarking, individuals can establish a structured organization for their online resources. This involves categorizing bookmarks into folders with clear labels, ensuring that each resource is easily identifiable. This organized approach not only saves time but also contributes to a more efficient workflow, especially for those engaged in academic research or professional tasks that require regular reference to specific online materials.

9.1.9.2 Staying Updated on Digital Trends:

FOLLOWING REPUTABLE Online Sources: Staying informed about digital trends is essential for effective online navigation. Users can identify and follow reputable online sources such as tech blogs, industry news websites, or official announcements from recognized organizations. Subscribing to newsletters or RSS feeds from these sources provides regular updates on the latest advancements, tools, and changes in the digital landscape.

Utilizing Social Media for Updates: Social media platforms can also serve as sources for staying updated on digital trends. Following industry experts, organizations, and relevant hashtags on platforms like Twitter or LinkedIn can provide real-time insights into emerging technologies, software updates, and noteworthy developments. However, it's crucial to verify information from multiple sources to ensure accuracy.

Engaging in Online Communities: Joining online communities, forums, or discussion groups related to specific fields or interests is another effective way to stay updated. These communities often share valuable insights, discuss emerging trends, and provide practical tips based on collective experiences. Active participation in these forums allows individuals to contribute to discussions and gain diverse perspectives on digital trends.

In conclusion, effective online navigation involves not only technical skills but also practical strategies for managing and staying informed about digital content. By adopting organized bookmarking practices and staying abreast of digital trends through reputable sources, individuals can enhance their online experience and maximize the benefits of the vast information available on the internet.

9.2 Overview of Online Research Tools:

9.2.1 Reference Management Software:

EXPLORING TOOLS LIKE EndNote, Zotero, or Mendeley: Reference management software plays a crucial role in academic research by helping users efficiently organize and cite sources. Tools like EndNote, Zotero, and Mendeley offer features such as automatic citation generation, bibliography creation, and the ability to organize references in a systematic manner. Researchers can save time and ensure accuracy in their citations, making these tools valuable assets for scholarly writing.

EndNote: EndNote allows users to collect and organize references, create bibliographies, and cite sources seamlessly. It integrates with various word processors, facilitating a smooth writing and citation process.

9.2.1.1 Zotero:

Figure 26:(*Zotero | Downloads, n.d.*)

ZOTERO IS A POWERFUL open-source reference management tool designed to assist researchers, students, and academics in efficiently collecting, organizing, and citing sources for their scholarly work. It provides a user-friendly platform for managing bibliographic data, storing research materials, and generating citations. Here's an overview of Zotero and a guide on how to install and use it:

Key Features of Zotero:

Reference Collection:

- Zotero allows users to collect and store references, including books, articles, websites, and more.
- It automatically extracts metadata from sources, making the organization of references seamless.

Browser Integration:

- Zotero offers browser extensions for popular web browsers like Chrome, Firefox, and Safari.

- Users can capture references directly from websites, databases, and online articles with a single click.

Document Organization:

- References can be organized into collections, allowing users to categorize and manage their sources effectively.
- Zotero also enables users to tag entries, facilitating advanced organization and retrieval.

Citation Styles:

- The tool supports a wide range of citation styles, including APA, MLA, Chicago, and more.
- Users can easily switch between citation styles and generate formatted bibliographies.

Collaboration:

- Zotero facilitates collaborative research by allowing users to share collections with team members.
- Shared collections can be accessed and edited by multiple users in real-time.

How to Install Zotero:

- ***Step 1: Download Zotero***

Visit the Zotero download page and select the appropriate version for your operating system (Windows, macOS, or Linux).

- ***Step 2: Install Zotero***

Follow the installation instructions provided on the Zotero download page.

Once installed, Zotero will prompt you to install the browser extension for your preferred browser.

- ***Step 3: Install Browser Extension***

Click on the Zotero icon in your browser and follow the instructions to install the browser extension.

- *Step 4: Create a Zotero Account (Optional)*

While not required, creating a Zotero account allows you to sync your library across multiple devices and collaborate with others.

- Step 5: Start Using Zotero

Open Zotero and begin adding references to your library using the browser extension or manually.

Organize your references into collections and use tags for efficient categorization.

- ***Step 6: Cite Sources in Documents***

Use Zotero's word processor plugins (available for Microsoft Word, LibreOffice, and Google Docs) to easily cite sources in your documents.

Select your preferred citation style, and Zotero will generate citations and bibliographies automatically.

Figure 27: Typical Zotero Interface showing references

Zotero's intuitive interface, extensive features, and collaborative capabilities make it a valuable tool for anyone engaged in academic or research-related work. Whether you are a student, researcher, or educator, Zotero can significantly streamline the process of managing and citing your references.

Figure 28: Mendeley download page

9.2.1.2
Mendeley:

MENDELEY IS A COMPREHENSIVE reference management tool that seamlessly blends reference organization with social networking features, fostering collaboration among researchers. Its capabilities extend beyond reference management, making it a valuable platform for academics, students, and professionals. Here are some key aspects of Mendeley:

Core Features:

Reference Management:

- Mendeley allows users to collect, organize, and manage their references effectively.
- References can be easily imported from various sources, including databases, websites, and PDFs.

PDF Annotation:

- One distinctive feature of Mendeley is its PDF annotation tool.
- Users can highlight, annotate, and add notes directly within PDF documents, streamlining the research review process.

Social Networking:

- Mendeley incorporates social networking features to facilitate collaboration and knowledge sharing among researchers.
- Users can connect with peers, join groups, and discover relevant research in their field.

Collaboration:

- Researchers can collaborate on shared projects, allowing for real-time collaboration on reference management and document writing.
- The collaboration features enhance teamwork and information exchange among research groups.

Discovery and Recommendation:

- Mendeley's social platform enables users to discover research articles and publications recommended by peers.
- The recommendation engine suggests relevant content based on a user's research interests and network activity.

How to Use Mendeley:

- ***Step 1: Create a Mendeley Account***

Visit the Mendeley website[1] and sign up for a Mendeley account.

- ***Step 2: Download and Install Mendeley Desktop***

Download the Mendeley Desktop application and follow the installation instructions.

- ***Step 3: Add References to Your Library***

Import references by adding them manually, importing from databases, or dragging and dropping PDFs into your Mendeley library.

- ***Step 4: Organize Your Library***

Create folders and tags to organize your references efficiently.
Use Mendeley's search and filter features to locate specific references.

- ***Step 5: Collaborate and Connect***

---

1. https://www.mendeley.com/

Connect with colleagues and peers on the Mendeley social platform.

Join relevant groups and participate in discussions to stay updated on current research.

- ***Step 6: Annotate PDFs***

Utilize Mendeley's PDF annotation tools to add comments, highlight text, and annotate research papers.

- ***Step 7: Insert Citations and Generate Bibliographies***

Use the Mendeley Cite-O-Matic plugin for Microsoft Word or LibreOffice to insert citations and generate bibliographies.

- ***Step 8: Sync Across Devices***

Sync your Mendeley library across multiple devices to access your references and annotations from anywhere.

Mendeley's unique combination of reference management, collaboration, and discovery features makes it a versatile tool for researchers looking to streamline their workflow and stay connected with the academic community. Whether you are working on individual projects or collaborating with a research team, Mendeley provides a robust platform for efficient and collaborative research.

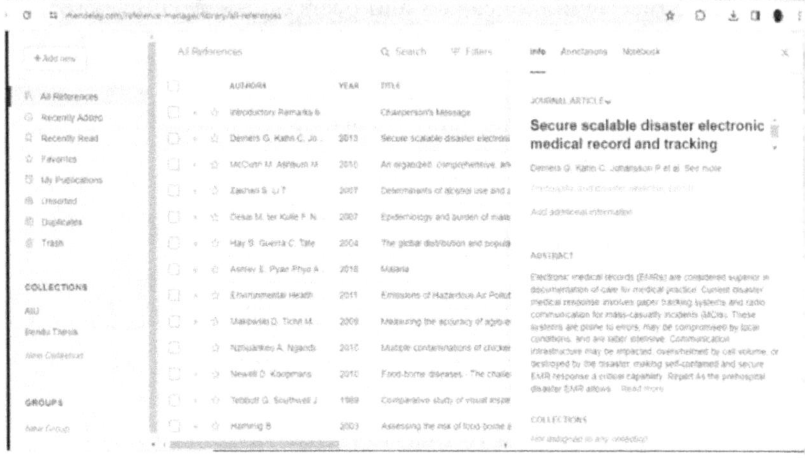

Figure 29: Typical interface of a Mendeley library

9.2.1.3 Collaborative Research Platforms:

PLATFORMS LIKE GOOGLE** Scholar and **ResearchGate:
Collaborative research platforms facilitate academic collaboration, information sharing, and networking among researchers. These platforms provide access to a vast repository of scholarly articles, research papers, and academic resources.

Figure 30:(*Google Scholar,* n.d.)

Google Scholar: Google Scholar is a freely accessible search engine that indexes scholarly articles, theses, books, conference papers, and patents. It provides a quick way to find academic sources and check citation metrics.

ResearchGate: ResearchGate is a professional network for researchers. It allows academics to share their publications, collaborate with peers, and connect with researchers globally. ResearchGate also provides features for asking and answering questions related to research.

Figure 31:(*ResearchGate | Find and Share Research, n.d.*)

THESE ONLINE RESEARCH tools contribute significantly to streamlining the research process, enhancing collaboration, and ensuring the quality and accuracy of academic work. Researchers can leverage these tools based on their specific needs and preferences, ultimately supporting a more efficient and productive research workflow.

Proficient online navigation skills are essential for academic success and lifelong learning. As you progress through this course, you will explore advanced features and applications of online resources. CIU envisions that this knowledge will empower you to navigate the digital landscape confidently, contributing to your success in academia and beyond. Let's continue this learning journey together!

9.3 Email Etiquette and Communication

WELCOME TO THE MODULE on "Email Etiquette and Communication" at CEPRES International University. In this session, we will delve into the essential principles of professional email communication. CIU recognizes the significance of effective email etiquette and aims to equip you with the skills needed for clear and professional digital communication.

9.3.1 Introduction to Email Etiquette:

9.3.1.1 Understanding the Importance of Email Etiquette:

EMAILS SERVE AS A PRIMARY means of professional and academic communication, making proper email etiquette essential for effective interaction. Email etiquette encompasses a set of guidelines that govern how emails should be composed, sent, and responded to. Adhering to these guidelines fosters clarity, professionalism, and positive relationships in both professional and academic settings.

9.3.1.2 Key Components of Email Etiquette:

FORMAL GREETINGS AND Closings:
Setting the Tone for Professional Communication: The salutation and closing of an email are crucial components that set the tone for professional communication. Starting with a formal greeting, such as "Dear [Recipient's Name]," and ending with a respectful closing, like "Sincerely" or "Best Regards," establishes a polite and professional atmosphere.

Clear and Concise Language:
Communicating Ideas Effectively: Email communication should be clear, concise, and focused. Avoiding unnecessary details and getting straight to the point enhances the recipient's understanding. Using proper grammar, punctuation, and spelling contributes to the professionalism of the message.

Professional Tone:

Maintaining a Polite and Respectful Tone: The tone of an email should remain professional, regardless of the nature of the communication. Politeness, respect, and a positive attitude contribute to building and maintaining professional relationships.

Subject Line Clarity:

Ensuring Readability and Relevance: A well-crafted subject line is crucial for grabbing the recipient's attention and providing a clear overview of the email's content. It helps recipients prioritize and understand the context of the message.

Consideration of Recipient's Time:

Respecting Time Constraints: Acknowledging that recipients may have busy schedules, emails should be crafted with brevity while ensuring all necessary information is included. Avoiding unnecessary back-and-forth emails contributes to efficiency.

Appropriate Use of Formatting:

Enhancing Readability: Proper formatting, including paragraphs, bullet points, and headings, improves the readability of emails. It allows recipients to grasp information quickly and facilitates a well-organized presentation.

Attachment Etiquette:

Clearly Indicating Attachments: When including attachments, it is essential to clearly mention them in the body of the email and ensure they are appropriately labeled. This prevents confusion and ensures that the recipient accesses the intended files.

Replying and Forwarding Etiquette:

Prompt and Thoughtful Responses: Timely responses to emails demonstrate professionalism and courtesy. When forwarding or replying, ensure that the email chain remains relevant, and provide context if necessary.

In summary, mastering email etiquette involves a combination of formalities, clarity, and consideration for the recipient. These principles contribute to effective communication, fostering positive professional and academic relationships.

9.3.2 Crafting Professional Emails:

9.3.2.1 Structuring Emails Effectively:

SUBJECT LINE IMPORTANCE:

- ***Ensuring Clarity in the Subject for Quick Understanding***: The subject line is the first thing recipients see, and it should succinctly convey the main purpose or topic of the email. A clear subject line aids quick comprehension and facilitates efficient email management.

Introduction and Body:

- ***Organizing Information Logically***: The introduction sets the tone for the email and should concisely state the purpose. The body of the email should be well-organized, presenting information logically. Use paragraphs and bullet points for clarity, ensuring the recipient can follow the message easily.

9.3.2.2 Addressing Recipients Appropriately:

USING PROPER SALUTATIONS:

- ***Tailoring Greetings Based on the Formality of the Communication***: The choice of salutation depends on the formality of the email and the relationship with the recipient. "Dear [Recipient's Name]" is appropriate for formal communication, while a more casual greeting may be suitable for colleagues or familiar contacts.

Addressing Multiple Recipients:

- ***Managing Group Emails Professionally***: When addressing multiple recipients, consider the nature of the communication. If the email is formal or professional, it's advisable to use a general salutation like "Dear Team" or "Hello All." If the email involves specific actions for individuals, mention their names explicitly.

9.3.2.3 Additional Tips for Crafting Professional Emails:

CLEAR AND CONCISE LANGUAGE:

- ***Avoiding Ambiguity and Redundancy***: Professional emails should be concise and to the point. Avoid unnecessary details that may lead to confusion. Be clear in your language, ensuring that the recipient easily grasps the purpose and action required.

Professional Tone:

- ***Maintaining a Respectful and Positive Tone***: Regardless of the content, maintaining a professional and respectful tone is essential. Avoid using language that may be interpreted as rude or offensive, and always express gratitude when appropriate.

Closing:

- ***Choosing Appropriate Closings***: The closing of the email should match the formality of the communication. "Sincerely" or "Best Regards" is suitable for formal emails, while a more casual closing like "Thank you" may be appropriate for internal communication.

Signature:

- ***Including a Professional Signature***: Conclude the email with a professional signature that includes your full name, job title, and contact information. This adds a level of formality and provides recipients with essential details for follow-up.

Crafting professional emails involves attention to detail in both structure and tone. A well-organized email with clear communication contributes to effective professional correspondence.

9.3.3 Tone and Language in Email Communication:

9.3.3.1 Choosing Appropriate Language:

PROFESSIONAL LANGUAGE Use:

- ***Avoiding Casual Language in Formal Communication***: In professional and academic settings, it's crucial to maintain a level of formality in email communication. Avoid overly casual language, abbreviations, or slang, especially when corresponding with superiors, colleagues, or external contacts.

Consideration of Cultural Differences:

- ***Adapting Language for Diverse Audiences***: Recognizing and respecting cultural differences is vital. Be mindful of language nuances that may have varying interpretations across cultures. Strive for clarity and inclusivity to ensure your message is well-received by a diverse audience.

9.3.3.2 Managing Tone in Emails:

AVOIDING MISINTERPRETATION:

- ***Clarifying Intentions to Prevent Misunderstandings***: Written communication lacks the non-verbal cues present in face-to-face interactions. To avoid misinterpretation, clearly express your intentions. If a message could be perceived differently than intended, consider providing context or asking for feedback to ensure mutual understanding.

Expressing Gratitude and Politeness:

- ***Enhancing the Overall Tone of the Email***: Regardless of the nature of the communication, incorporating expressions of gratitude and politeness contributes to a positive tone. Simple gestures like thanking the recipient for their time or assistance can foster goodwill and professionalism.

9.3.3.3 Tips for Maintaining Appropriate Tone and Language:

KNOW YOUR AUDIENCE:

- ***Understanding the Recipient's Expectations***: Tailor your language and tone based on your audience. Consider the recipient's position, familiarity, and cultural background. Adapting your communication style to align with the expectations of the recipient enhances effective communication.

Use Formal Greetings and Closings:

- ***Setting a Professional Tone from the Start***: Begin your email with a formal greeting and end it with an appropriate closing. This establishes a professional tone and reinforces the formality of the communication.

Review and Edit:

- ***Ensuring Clarity and Professionalism***: Before sending an email, review and edit your message. Ensure that the language is clear, professional, and free of any potential misunderstandings. This extra step helps maintain a polished and respectful tone.

Seek Feedback:

- ***Welcoming Input on Tone and Language***: If in doubt, seek feedback from colleagues or mentors. Another perspective can provide valuable insights into how your email may be perceived and help you make necessary adjustments.

Effectively managing tone and language in email communication is essential for conveying messages accurately and maintaining professional relationships. By being mindful of cultural considerations and adapting your language to the context, you enhance the effectiveness of your written correspondence.

9.3.4 Email Response Etiquette:

9.3.4.1 Timely Responses:

PROMPT EMAIL REPLIES:

- ***Acknowledging Emails in a Timely Manner***: Responding promptly to emails demonstrates professionalism and courtesy. Aim to acknowledge receipt of emails, especially those requiring a more detailed response, in a timely manner.

Setting Expectations for Response Time:

- ***Communicating Availability***: When appropriate, communicate your expected response time. If you are unable to reply promptly, setting clear expectations helps manage the sender's anticipation and avoids misunderstandings.

9.3.4.2 Out-of-Office Messages:

PROPER USAGE AND CONTENT:

- ***Crafting Informative Out-of-Office Messages***: When you're away from work or unavailable to respond to emails, activate an out-of-office message. Craft a clear and concise message indicating your unavailability, the reason (if necessary), and the expected duration of your absence.

Providing Alternative Contacts:

- ***Ensuring Continuity in Communication***: In out-of-office messages, consider providing alternative contacts or directing the sender to someone who can assist in your absence. This ensures that urgent matters can be addressed promptly, contributing to seamless communication.

9.3.4.3 Tips for Effective Email Responses:

PRIORITIZE RESPONSES:

- ***Addressing Urgent Matters First***: If you receive emails with varying levels of urgency, prioritize responses accordingly. Attend to urgent matters promptly, even if a more comprehensive response to other emails may take longer.

Be Clear and Concise:

- ***Maintaining Clarity in Responses***: When replying to emails, be clear and concise in your responses. Address the main points, provide relevant information, and avoid unnecessary details to ensure effective communication.

Express Gratitude:

- ***Acknowledging Politeness and Professionalism***: Express gratitude for emails that require acknowledgment or appreciation. A simple "Thank you for reaching out" or "I appreciate your prompt response" contributes to a positive email exchange.

Follow-Up Appropriately:

- ***Ensuring Follow-Up on Action Items***: If an email requires subsequent actions, ensure timely follow-up. Clearly communicate any necessary steps, deadlines, or expectations to maintain a smooth workflow.

Avoid Ambiguity:

- ***Clarifying Ambiguous Requests***: If an email contains ambiguous or unclear information, seek clarification before responding. This helps prevent misunderstandings and ensures that your responses are accurate and relevant.

Maintaining email response etiquette involves a combination of promptness, clear communication, and professionalism. By adhering to these guidelines, you contribute to effective and courteous email interactions, fostering positive relationships in professional and academic settings.

9.3.5 Managing Email Attachments:

EFFECTIVE USE OF ATTACHMENTS:

- *Naming Conventions*: Providing clear and relevant file names.
- *Attachment Size Considerations*: Avoiding large attachments when unnecessary.

9.3.6 Netiquette and Online Communication Guidelines:

9.3.6.1 Adhering to Netiquette:

OBSERVING PROFESSIONAL Conduct Online:

- *Respecting Others in Digital Communication*: Netiquette, or internet etiquette, emphasizes the importance of maintaining respect and courtesy in online interactions. When engaging in digital communication, whether through emails, forums, or social media, adhere to the same level of professionalism as in face-to-face interactions.

Avoiding All Caps and Excessive Punctuation:

- *Maintaining Readability*: Writing in all capital letters is considered the online equivalent of shouting and can be perceived as impolite. Additionally, excessive use of punctuation marks, especially exclamation points, may convey an unintended tone. It's crucial to strike a balance and use appropriate punctuation for clear and respectful communication.

9.3.6.2 Additional Guidelines for Netiquette:

MINDFUL LANGUAGE USE:

- ***Choosing Words Wisely***: Be mindful of the language you use in online communication. Avoid offensive or inappropriate language, and ensure that your words accurately convey your intended meaning. Consider the potential impact of your message on the recipient.

Be Clear and Concise:

- ***Conveying Messages Clearly***: In written communication, clarity is essential. Craft messages that are clear, concise, and directly convey your intended message. Ambiguity can lead to misunderstandings, so strive for straightforward and effective communication.

Avoiding Overuse of Emoticons:

- ***Using Emoticons Sparingly***: Emoticons, such as smiley faces or thumbs up, can add a touch of informality and convey emotions in online communication. However, overusing them may detract from professionalism. Use emoticons judiciously, especially in formal or academic settings.

Respecting Privacy and Confidentiality:

- ***Exercise Caution with Sensitive Information***: Be mindful of privacy and confidentiality. Avoid sharing sensitive or personal information in public forums or emails unless absolutely necessary. Respect the privacy of others by refraining from sharing their private information without consent.

Responding Appropriately to Criticism:

- ***Handling Criticism Professionally***: In online discussions, disagreements may arise. When faced with criticism or differing opinions, respond professionally and constructively. Avoid engaging in heated arguments, and focus on maintaining a respectful and open dialogue.

Acknowledging Receipt of Emails:

- ***Confirming Receipt of Important Emails***: When receiving important emails, especially in professional or academic settings, acknowledge receipt. A simple "Thank you for your email, I have received it" lets the sender know their message reached you.

Encouraging Inclusive Communication:

- ***Promoting Inclusivity and Diversity***: Foster an inclusive online environment by recognizing and respecting diversity. Be mindful of cultural differences and avoid making assumptions. Encourage open and inclusive communication.

Adhering to netiquette ensures that online communication remains respectful, effective, and conducive to positive interactions.

Following these guidelines contributes to a collaborative and courteous online environment.

9.3.7 Cybersecurity Awareness in Email Communication:

9.3.7.1 Recognizing Email Scams and Phishing:

IDENTIFYING SUSPICIOUS Emails:

- ***Common Signs of Phishing Attempts***: Be vigilant for emails exhibiting signs of phishing, such as:
    - ***Generic Greetings***: Phishing emails often use generic greetings like "Dear User" or "Dear Customer" instead of addressing you by name.
    - ***Urgent Language***: Phishing emails create a sense of urgency, urging immediate action to trick recipients into responding without thinking.
    - ***Unusual Sender Addresses***: Examine sender email addresses closely, especially if they seem unfamiliar or use variations of legitimate addresses.
    - ***Mismatched URLs***: Hover over links in emails to preview the destination URL. Phishing emails may include deceptive links that lead to malicious sites.

Verifying Sender Information:

- ***Ensuring Legitimacy of Email Content:*** Before clicking on any links or providing sensitive information, verify the legitimacy of the sender. Check for:
- ***Legitimate Sender Addresses***: Authentic emails come from recognized addresses associated with the organization or individual.

- ***Contacting the Sender***: If in doubt, contact the supposed sender through a separate, trusted communication channel to confirm the legitimacy of the email.

Avoiding Clicking on Suspicious Links:

- ***Hovering Over Links***: Hover over links without clicking to preview the destination URL. If the link appears suspicious or does not match the expected address, avoid clicking.

Verifying Email Requests for Information:

- ***Contacting the Organization Directly***: If an email requests sensitive information or actions, independently verify the request by contacting the organization directly through trusted channels. Avoid using contact details provided in the suspicious email.

Checking for Spelling and Grammar Errors:

- Phishing emails often contain spelling and grammar errors. Genuine communications from reputable sources typically undergo thorough proofreading, making such errors a red flag for potential phishing attempts.

Being Skeptical of Unexpected Attachments:

- ***Attachments from Unknown Sources***: Exercise caution when opening attachments, especially if they come from unexpected or unknown sources. Malicious attachments can contain harmful software.

Enabling Two-Factor Authentication:

- ***Enhancing Security Measures***: Enable two-factor authentication (2FA) on email accounts when possible. 2FA adds an extra layer of security by requiring additional verification beyond a password.

Reporting Suspected Phishing Attempts:

- ***Alerting IT or Security Teams***: If you receive an email that appears to be a phishing attempt, report it to your IT or security teams. They can investigate and take necessary measures to protect against potential threats.

Staying informed about common phishing tactics and being cautious in email communication helps mitigate cybersecurity risks. Regularly update security software, stay vigilant for phishing indicators, and follow best practices to enhance email communication security.

9.3.8 Practical Tips for Effective Email Communication:

9.3.8.1 Proofreading and Editing:

CHECKING FOR GRAMMATICAL Errors:

- ***Importance of Clarity***: Before sending an email, carefully review the content for grammatical errors. Clear and well-written emails enhance professionalism and avoid misinterpretations.
- ***Grammar and Punctuation***: Pay attention to proper grammar and punctuation, as errors can impact the professionalism of the communication.

Ensuring Clarity Before Sending:

- ***Effective Communication***: Ensure that your email conveys the intended message clearly. Ambiguity can lead to misunderstandings, so be concise and articulate in your writing.
- ***Avoiding Jargon***: Minimize the use of technical jargon or industry-specific terms that may not be familiar to all recipients.

9.3.8.2 Using Email Signatures:

CREATING PROFESSIONAL Email Signatures:

- ***Including Contact Information***: Craft a professional email signature that includes your full name, job title, company or affiliation, and contact details.
- ***Consistency Across Platforms:*** Ensure consistency in your email signature across different platforms and devices for a cohesive and professional appearance.
- ***Optional Additional Information***: Consider including relevant links to your professional profiles or a brief, informative tagline.

Adding Legal Disclaimers or Company Policies:

- ***Compliance and Consistency***: If applicable, include legal disclaimers or links to company policies in your email signature to ensure compliance and maintain consistency across communications.

Using Professional Fonts and Formatting:

- *Font Selection*: Choose professional and easily readable fonts for your email content and signature. Avoid overly decorative or informal fonts in professional communications.
- *Consistent Formatting*: Maintain consistent formatting throughout your email, including font size and style, to present a polished and organized appearance.

Avoiding Excessive Formatting:

- *Simple and Clean Design*: Keep the design of your email and signature simple and clean. Avoid excessive formatting, colors, or fonts that may distract from the content.

Including Relevant Social Media Links:

- *Optional Social Media Presence*: If appropriate for your professional context, consider including links to relevant social media profiles. Ensure these profiles present a consistent and professional image.

Mobile-Friendly Signatures:

- *Adapting to Mobile Devices*: Optimize your email signature for mobile devices, ensuring that it remains clear and professional when viewed on smaller screens.

By incorporating these practical tips, individuals can enhance the professionalism, clarity, and overall effectiveness of their email communication. Consistent proofreading, attention to detail, and a well-crafted email signature contribute to positive and impactful professional interactions.

9.3.9 Overview of Email Platforms:

EMAIL PLATFORMS PLAY a crucial role in facilitating digital communication, providing users with a variety of features and functionalities. Below is an overview of some popular email platforms:

Gmail:

- *User-Friendly Interface*: Gmail, developed by Google, is known for its intuitive and user-friendly interface.
- *Integrated Services*: It seamlessly integrates with other Google services such as Google Drive, Google Calendar, and Hangouts.
- *Powerful Search Capabilities*: Gmail offers powerful search capabilities, making it easy to locate specific emails.

Outlook:

- *Microsoft Integration*: Outlook is part of the Microsoft Office suite, making it well-integrated with other Microsoft applications.
- *Advanced Organization Features*: It provides advanced email organization features, including folders, categories, and rules.
- *Calendar and Task Integration*: Outlook includes a calendar and task management system, enhancing productivity.

Yahoo Mail:

- *Long-Standing Provider*: Yahoo Mail has been a long-standing email service provider.
- *Clean Interface*: It offers a clean and straightforward interface with customizable themes.
- *Generous Storage*: Yahoo Mail provides ample storage space for emails and attachments.

Apple Mail:

- ***Native to Apple Devices***: Apple Mail is the default email client on Apple devices such as iPhones and Mac computers.
- ***Seamless Integration***: It integrates well with other Apple applications and services.
- ***Synchronization Across Devices***: Emails, contacts, and settings are synchronized across Apple devices using iCloud.

ProtonMail:

- ***Focus on Security***: ProtonMail is known for its emphasis on privacy and security.
- End-to-End Encryption: It offers end-to-end encryption for enhanced email security.
- ***Anonymous Account Creation***: Users can create accounts without providing personally identifiable information.

Zoho Mail:

- ***Business-Focused***: Zoho Mail caters to business users with a suite of collaboration and productivity tools.
- ***Custom Domain Support***: It allows users to use custom domains for a professional email address.
- ***Calendar and Collaboration***: Zoho Mail integrates with Zoho Calendar and other business applications.

Thunderbird:

- ***Open-Source:*** Thunderbird is an open-source email client developed by Mozilla.
- ***Customizable and Extensible***: It is highly customizable with various add-ons and extensions available.

- ***Cross-Platform Support***: Thunderbird is compatible with multiple operating systems, providing flexibility for users.

These platforms offer diverse features and cater to different user preferences and needs. The choice of an email platform often depends on individual preferences, professional requirements, and the specific features offered by each service.

Mastering email etiquette is a fundamental skill for successful academic and professional communication. As you progress through this course, you will gain advanced insights into managing various aspects of email communication. CIU envisions that this knowledge will empower you to navigate the digital communication landscape with confidence and professionalism. Let's continue this learning journey together!

Figure 32: Video/Audio conferencing interface

Introduction to Video Conferencing Tools

10.1 Microsoft Teams

WELCOME TO THE MODULE on "Microsoft Teams" at CEPRES International University. In this session, we will explore the functionalities and features of Microsoft Teams, a powerful tool for virtual collaboration and communication. CIU recognizes the importance of effective team collaboration, and this module aims to equip you with the skills needed to leverage Microsoft Teams for academic and professional success.

10.1.1 Introduction to Microsoft Teams:

UNDERSTANDING MICROSOFT Teams:

- Microsoft Teams is a collaborative platform integrating chat, video conferencing, file storage, and application integration.
- It is designed to enhance communication and collaboration within teams.

Importance of Microsoft Teams:

- Virtual Collaboration: Facilitating teamwork in both remote and in-person settings.
- Integration with Microsoft 365: Seamless connectivity with other Microsoft applications.

10.1.2 Features and Functions:

CHAT AND MESSAGING:

- Individual and Group Chats: Communicating with team members privately or in groups.
- Emoji and GIF Integration: Adding a dynamic element to messages.

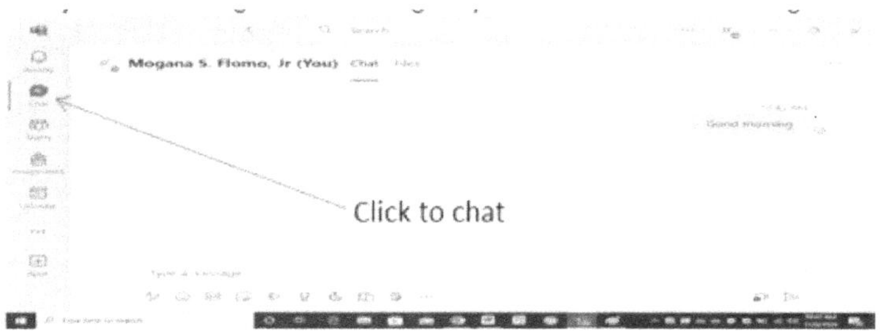

Figure 33: Showing where to chat from

File Sharing and Collaboration:

- Uploading and Sharing Documents: Collaborating on files in real-time.
- Version History: Tracking changes and revisions in shared documents.

. . . .

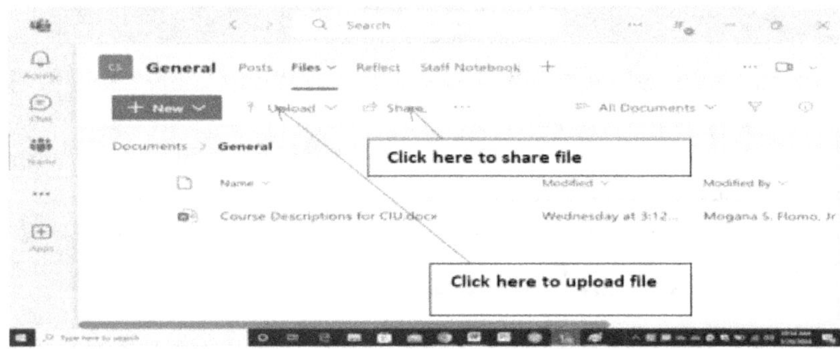

Figure 34: File sharing screen

MEETINGS AND VIDEO Conferencing:

- Scheduling and Joining Meetings: Setting up virtual meetings with ease.
- Video and Audio Settings: Configuring preferences for a seamless meeting experience.

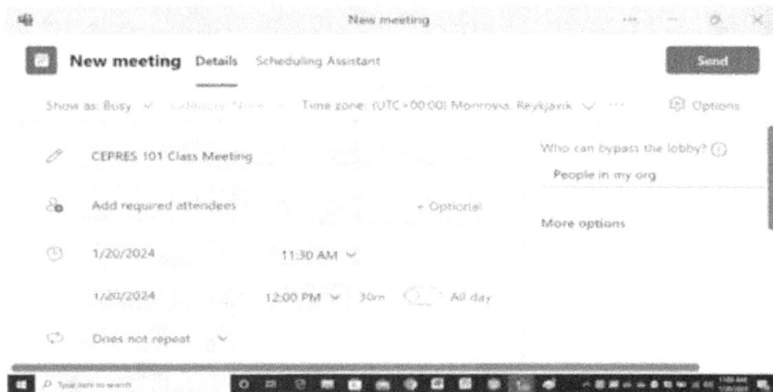

Figure 35: Set meeting time, invite attendees and more on this screen

Channel Organization:

- Creating and Managing Channels: Organizing discussions and files by topics.

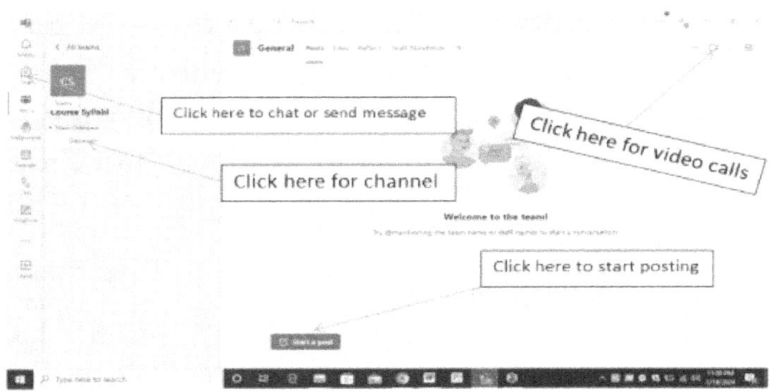

Figure 36: Microsoft Teams showing importnat features

- Channel Tabs: Customizing channels with specific applications and tools.

10.1.3 Tips for Effective Collaboration:

MICROSOFT TEAMS IS a powerful collaboration platform, and optimizing its features can significantly enhance teamwork. Here are some tips for effective collaboration on Microsoft Teams:

Presence and Status Settings:

- ***Indicating Availability***: Use Teams' presence settings to communicate your availability to your team. Set your status to "Available," "Busy," or "Do Not Disturb" to provide real-time information about your accessibility.
- ***Status Updates:*** Utilize status updates to share information on your current activities. This brief status message helps colleagues understand your focus or inform them of your tasks.

Notification Management:

- ***Customizing Notification Preferences***: Adjust your notification settings to align with your work preferences. Customize how and when you receive notifications to avoid unnecessary interruptions during focused work periods.

- **@*Mentions and Alerts***: Stay attentive to @mentions and alerts, as these are used to draw attention to specific messages or tasks. Respond promptly to messages that directly involve you.

Clear Communication:

- ***Use Conversations Effectively***: Utilize Teams' conversation features for clear and threaded discussions. Keep messages concise and organized, and use threaded replies when discussing specific topics.
- ***Share Context***: When posting messages or sharing files, provide sufficient context to help team members understand the purpose and relevance of the information.

File Organization and Sharing:

- **Utilize SharePoint Integration**: Teams integrates with SharePoint for file storage. Leverage this integration to organize and share files seamlessly. Ensure that documents are stored in channels or folders with logical structures.
- ***Coauthoring in Real-Time***: Take advantage of Teams' real-time coauthoring feature when working on documents. This promotes simultaneous collaboration and ensures everyone is on the same page.

Effective Meeting Management:

- ***Schedule Efficient Meetings***: When scheduling meetings, provide clear agendas and objectives. Use the meeting features, such as screen sharing and collaboration on documents, to make virtual meetings more interactive.

- ***Recording Meetings***: Consider recording meetings to allow absent team members to catch up on discussions and decisions.

Task Management:

- ***Use Planner or To-Do Integration***: Microsoft Teams integrates with Planner and To-Do for task management. Utilize these integrations to create, assign, and track tasks directly within Teams.
- ***Kanban Boards***: If applicable, set up Kanban boards within Teams for visualizing and managing tasks using boards, lists, and cards.

Encourage Open Communication:

- ***Open Channels for Discussion***: Create open channels for general discussions, fostering a sense of community and collaboration. This can be a space for non-work-related conversations.
- ***Encourage Feedback***: Create an environment where team members feel comfortable providing feedback. Use Teams for both formal and informal feedback loops.

Security and Compliance:

- ***Educate Team Members***: Ensure that team members are educated on security and compliance features in Teams. Emphasize the importance of following security best practices, especially when handling sensitive information.

Training and Support:

- ***Continuous Training***: Regularly update team members on new features and functionalities in Teams through training sessions. This ensures that everyone is making the most of the platform.
- ***Provide Support Channels***: Establish channels or resources for team members to seek help or clarification regarding Teams-related issues.

By incorporating these tips into your Microsoft Teams collaboration strategy, you can create a more efficient and streamlined teamwork experience for your organization.

10.1.4 Security and Privacy Considerations:

DATA ENCRYPTION AND Compliance:

- End-to-End Encryption: Understanding the security of your communications.
- Compliance Features: Ensuring adherence to regulatory standards.

Controlling Access and Permissions:

- User Roles: Managing roles and permissions within teams.
- Guest Access: Allowing external collaborators with controlled permissions.

10.1.5 Integrations with Other Tools:

MICROSOFT 365 INTEGRATION:

- Seamless Connectivity: Linking Teams with applications like Word, Excel, and PowerPoint.
- OneNote and Planner Integration: Streamlining project

management within Teams.

10.1.6 Best Practices for Microsoft Teams:

ESTABLISHING TEAM GUIDELINES:

- Creating a Code of Conduct: Setting expectations for communication and collaboration.
- Regular Check-Ins: Ensuring effective team communication and coordination.

10.1.7 Troubleshooting Common Issues:

10.1.7.1 Troubleshooting Common Issues in Microsoft Teams:

MICROSOFT TEAMS IS a powerful collaboration tool, but like any software, users may encounter occasional issues. Here are some tips for troubleshooting common problems related to connection, audio, and video:

Connection Problems:

- ***Check Internet Connection***: Ensure that your internet connection is stable. If possible, use a wired connection for better reliability.
- ***Restart Teams***: Close and reopen the Teams application. This simple step can resolve many connectivity issues.
- ***Check Firewall and Antivirus Settings***: Verify that your firewall or antivirus software is not blocking Teams. Adjust settings if necessary.

10.1.7.2 Audio/Video Problems:

CHECK MICROPHONE AND Camera Settings:

- Ensure that your microphone and camera are properly connected.
- Check Teams settings to ensure the correct microphone and camera are selected.

Adjust Audio and Video Settings in a Meeting:

- During a meeting, click on the ellipsis (three dots) and select "Device settings" to adjust audio and video settings.
- Test the settings before joining a meeting to ensure everything is working as expected.

Update Audio/Video Drivers:

- Ensure that your device's audio and video drivers are up-to-date.
- Check the manufacturer's website for driver updates.

Basic Troubleshooting Steps:

- Restart Device: A simple restart can often resolve various software and hardware issues.

10.1.7.3 Clear Teams Cache:

CLOSE TEAMS.

- Go to the system tray, right-click the Teams icon, and select "Quit."
- Relaunch Teams. This clears the cache and can resolve some performance issues.

Update Teams:

- Make sure you are using the latest version of Teams. Updates often include bug fixes and improvements.

Microsoft Support Resources:

- ***Teams Help Center***: Visit the Microsoft Teams Help Center for comprehensive guides and troubleshooting resources.
- ***Community Forums***: Explore the Microsoft Teams Community for discussions and solutions provided by other Teams users.
- ***Contact Support***: If the issue persists, contact Microsoft Support through the Teams support page for personalized assistance.

Check Service Status:

- Visit the Microsoft 365 Service Status[1] page to check if there are any ongoing issues with Teams. Microsoft regularly updates this page with information on service disruptions.

Figure 37: Microsoft Teams App Icon

By following these troubleshooting steps and utilizing Microsoft's support resources, users can address common issues and ensure a smoother experience with Microsoft Teams.

---

1. https://status.office.com/

10.1.8 Overview of Microsoft Teams Mobile App:

MICROSOFT TEAMS PROVIDES a mobile application that extends collaboration capabilities to smartphones and tablets. Here is an overview of accessing Teams on mobile devices, including downloading and installing the app, as well as exploring mobile-specific features and functions:

10.1.8.1 Downloading and Installing the Mobile App:

PLATFORM COMPATIBILITY: The Microsoft Teams mobile app is available for both iOS and Android platforms. Users can download it from the respective app stores: App Store for iOS and Google Play for Android.

Installation: After downloading the app, follow the on-screen instructions to install it on your mobile device.

Mobile Features and Functions:

- ***User Interface***: The mobile app provides a streamlined interface designed for smaller screens, ensuring a user-friendly experience on smartphones and tablets.

Chat and Messaging:

- Users can engage in individual and group chats, send multimedia files, and use emojis and GIFs for expressive communication.
- Access to threaded conversations allows for organized discussions.

Meetings and Calls:

- Join scheduled meetings or initiate impromptu video and

audio calls from the mobile app.

- Participate in video conferences, share your screen, and collaborate on documents during meetings.

Collaboration Tools:

- Access and collaborate on shared files and documents using mobile-friendly views.
- Use real-time editing and commenting features for collaborative work on the go.

Notifications and Alerts:

- Receive push notifications for new messages, mentions, and upcoming meetings.
- Stay informed about updates and activities within Teams through mobile alerts.

Activity Feed:

- The activity feed provides a chronological view of recent interactions, ensuring users don't miss important updates.

Integration with Mobile Functions:

- Leverage device-specific functions such as camera, microphone, and location services for enhanced collaboration.
- Integrate Teams with other mobile apps for a seamless workflow.

By downloading the Microsoft Teams mobile app, users can stay connected and collaborate from anywhere, extending the reach of

Teams beyond traditional desktop environments. The mobile application is designed to provide a rich set of features tailored for on-the-go productivity and efficient communication on various mobile devices.

Microsoft Teams is a versatile platform that can significantly enhance collaborative efforts. As you progress through this course, you will gain practical insights into maximizing the potential of Microsoft Teams for academic and professional purposes. CIU envisions that this knowledge will empower you to excel in virtual teamwork and communication. Let's continue this learning journey together!

10.2 Zoom

WELCOME TO THE MODULE on "Zoom" at CEPRES International University. In this session, we will explore the functionalities and features of Zoom, a widely used video conferencing platform. CIU acknowledges the importance of virtual meetings, classes and collaboration, and this module aims to equip you with the skills needed to effectively utilize Zoom for academic and professional purposes.

10.2.1 Introduction to Zoom:

UNDERSTANDING ZOOM:

- Zoom is a cloud-based video conferencing platform that allows users to conduct virtual meetings, webinars, and collaborative sessions.
- It is widely known for its user-friendly interface and versatile features.

Importance of Zoom in Modern Communication:

- Virtual Meetings and classes: Facilitating real-time

communication irrespective of geographical locations.

- Webinars and Workshops: Hosting interactive online events.

10.2.2 Features and Functions:

SCHEDULING AND JOINING Meetings:

- Creating and Sending Invitations: Setting up meetings and inviting participants.
- Joining Meetings: Understanding different methods of joining Zoom sessions.

Video and Audio Controls:

- Camera and Microphone Settings: Configuring video and audio preferences.
- Virtual Backgrounds: Customizing your environment during video calls.

Screen Sharing and Collaboration:

- Sharing Screens: Presenting documents, slides, or applications.
- Annotation and Whiteboard Features: Collaborating in real-time.

Breakout Rooms:

- Facilitating Group Discussions: Creating smaller discussion spaces within a larger meeting.
- Managing Breakout Sessions: Coordinating activities in separate rooms.

10.2.3 Tips for Effective Collaboration:

MEETING ETIQUETTE:

- Video On/Off Protocol: Guidelines for when to have video on or off.
- Muting and Unmuting: Ensuring clear communication during meetings.

Interactive Features:

- Q&A and Chat Functions: Engaging participants through chat and question sessions.
- Reactions and Emoticons: Adding expressions to virtual communication.

10.2.4 Security and Privacy Considerations:

MEETING ROOM SECURITY:

- Password Protection: Securing meetings with access codes.
- Waiting Rooms: Monitoring and admitting participants for added security.

Recording and Storing Meetings:

- Recording Meetings: Capturing sessions for future reference.
- Managing and Sharing Recorded Sessions: Accessing recorded content.

10.2.5 Integrations with Other Tools:

CALENDAR INTEGRATIONS:

- Syncing with Calendar Apps: Connecting Zoom with

calendars for efficient scheduling.

- Automatic Meeting Reminders: Streamlining meeting notifications.

10.2.6 Best Practices for Zoom:

PRE-MEETING PREPARATIONS:

- Testing Audio and Video: Ensuring equipment readiness before meetings.
- Setting Agendas: Clarifying objectives for more focused discussions.

10.2.7 Troubleshooting Common Issues:

CONNECTION AND AUDIO/Video Problems:

- Basic Troubleshooting Steps: Resolving common technical challenges.
- Zoom Support Resources: Accessing online support for more complex issues.

10.2.8 Overview of Zoom Mobile App:

ACCESSING ZOOM ON MOBILE Devices:

- Downloading and Installing the Mobile App: Extending Zoom capabilities to smartphones and tablets.
- Mobile Features and Functions: Exploring mobile-specific functionalities.

Zoom is a versatile platform that enhances virtual communication and collaboration. As you progress through this course, you will gain practical insights into maximizing the potential of Zoom for academic and professional purposes. CIU envisions that this knowledge will empower you to excel in virtual meetings and collaboration. Let's continue this learning journey together!

10.3 Google Meet

WELCOME TO THE MODULE on "Google Meet" at CEPRES International University. In this session, we will explore the functionalities and features of Google Meet, a powerful video conferencing platform. CIU recognizes the significance of seamless collaboration, and this module aims to equip you with the skills needed to effectively use Google Meet for academic and professional purposes.

10.3.1 Introduction to Google Meet:

UNDERSTANDING GOOGLE Meet:

- Google Meet is a web-based video conferencing platform developed by Google, providing a platform for virtual meetings, collaboration, and communication.

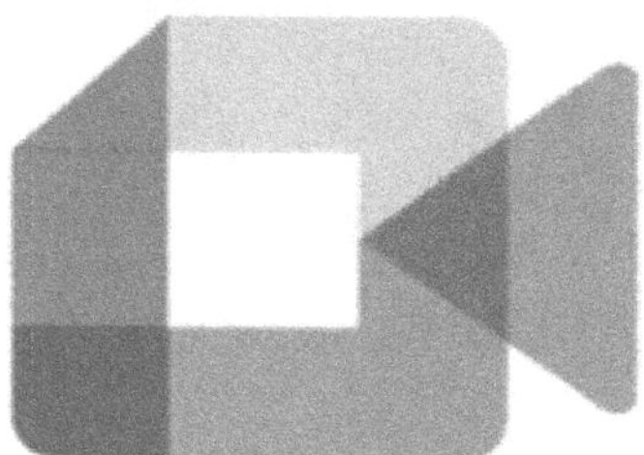

Figure 38: Google Met Icon

- It is integrated with Google Workspace, making it a versatile tool for users familiar with Google's ecosystem.

Importance of Google Meet:

- Integration with Google Services: Seamlessly connected with Google Calendar, Gmail, and other Google applications.

- Ease of Use: User-friendly interface for effective virtual meetings.

10.3.2 Features and Functions:

GOOGLE MEET PROVIDES a variety of features and functions to facilitate effective virtual meetings. Here's an overview of key functionalities:

10.3.2.1 Scheduling and Joining Meetings:

CREATING MEETINGS THROUGH Google Calendar:

- Google Meet integrates seamlessly with Google Calendar, allowing users to schedule meetings directly from the calendar interface.

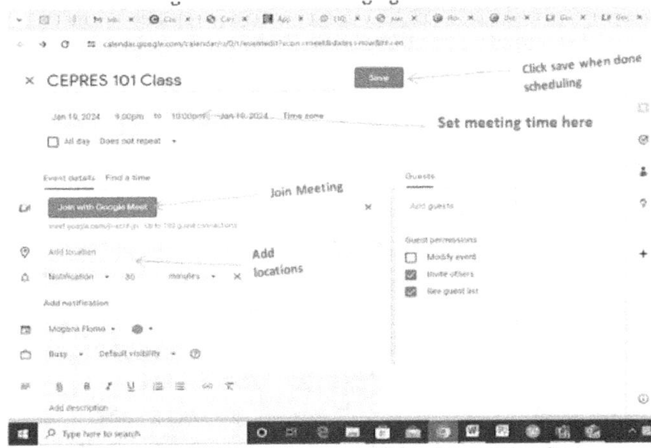

Figure 39: Showing how to schedule a Teams Meeting

- This integration streamlines the scheduling process, making it convenient for users who use Google Calendar for managing their schedules.

Joining Meetings through Email Invitations:

- Participants can easily join scheduled meetings by clicking on the link provided in email invitations.
- This straightforward process ensures quick and easy access for participants without requiring complex steps.

10.3.2.2 Video and Audio Controls:

ENABLING AND DISABLING Camera/Microphone:

- Participants have control over their video and audio settings, allowing them to enable or disable their cameras and microphones as needed.
- This feature provides flexibility and privacy during meetings.

Adjusting Bandwidth Settings:

- Google Meet allows participants to adjust bandwidth settings to ensure a smooth meeting experience, especially in situations where bandwidth may be limited or variable.

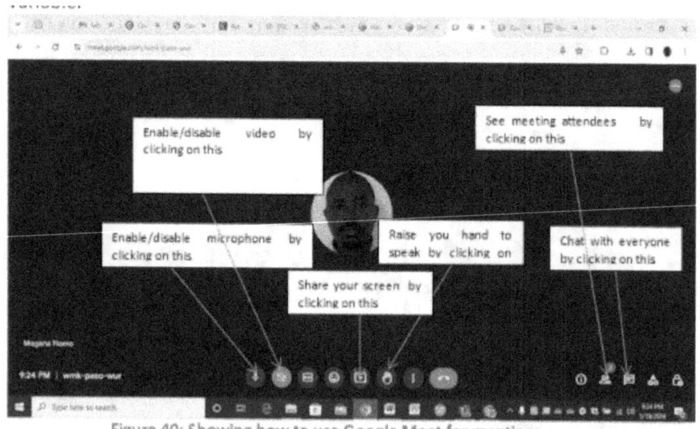

Figure 40: Showing how to use Google Meet for meetings

10.3.2.3 Screen Sharing and Collaboration:

SHARING SCREENS:

- Participants can share their screens, enabling the presentation of documents, slides, or applications.
- Screen sharing enhances collaborative discussions and presentations.

Real-time Collaboration:

- Google Meet supports real-time collaboration, allowing participants to edit shared documents during the meeting.
- This feature promotes collaborative work and discussions directly within the meeting platform.

Google Meet's features collectively contribute to creating a dynamic and interactive virtual meeting environment. Whether scheduling, adjusting settings, or collaborating in real-time, Google Meet provides a robust set of tools for efficient online meetings and collaboration.

10.3.3 Tips for Effective Collaboration:

MEETING ETIQUETTE:

- Muting and Unmuting Guidelines: Managing audio for clear communication.
- Using Reactions and Emoji: Adding expressions in a virtual setting.

Interactive Features:

- Q&A and Chat Functions: Facilitating engagement through

questions and chat.
- Attendance Tracking: Monitoring participant attendance.

10.3.4 Security and Privacy Considerations:

MEETING CONTROLS AND Security Options:

- Control Over Entry and Exit: Managing participant access during meetings.
- End-to-End Encryption: Ensuring secure communication.

Recording and Storage:

- Recording Meetings: Capturing sessions for future reference.
- Accessing and Sharing Recorded Sessions: Utilizing recorded content.

10.3.5 Integration with Other Tools:

GOOGLE WORKSPACE INTEGRATION:

- Connected with Google Docs, Sheets, and Slides: Enhancing collaborative work during meetings.
- Calendar Integration: Syncing schedules for efficient meeting planning.

10.3.6 Best Practices for Google Meet:

PRE-MEETING PREPARATION:

- Testing Audio/Video Before Meetings: Ensuring equipment readiness.
- Setting Agendas: Clarifying objectives for focused discussions.

10.3.7 Troubleshooting Common Issues:

CONNECTION AND AUDIO/Video Problems:

- Basic Troubleshooting Steps: Resolving common technical challenges.
- Google Meet Support Resources: Accessing online support for more complex issues.

10.3.8 Overview of Google Meet Mobile App:

ACCESSING GOOGLE MEET on Mobile Devices:

- Downloading and Installing the Mobile App: Extending Google Meet capabilities to smartphones and tablets.
- Mobile Features and Functions: Exploring mobile-specific functionalities.

Google Meet is a versatile tool for virtual collaboration, providing a seamless experience for online meetings. As you progress through this course, you will gain practical insights into maximizing the potential of Google Meet for academic and professional purposes. CIU envisions that this knowledge will empower you to excel in virtual collaboration and communication. Let's continue this learning journey together!

11 Collaborative Tools and Project Management

11.1 Google Docs, Sheets, and Slides

WELCOME TO THE MODULE on "Google Docs, Sheets, and Slides" at CEPRES International University. In this session, we will explore the versatile suite of applications provided by Google for document creation, data analysis, and presentation development. CIU recognizes the importance of collaborative tools, and this module aims to equip you with the skills needed to effectively use Google Docs, Sheets, and Slides for academic and professional purposes.

11.1.1 Introduction to Google Docs, Sheets, and Slides:

UNDERSTANDING GOOGLE Workspace:

- Google Workspace is a suite of cloud computing, productivity, and collaboration tools developed by Google.
- Google Docs, Sheets, and Slides are key components of this suite, providing online alternatives to traditional office applications.

11.1.2 Google Docs: Document Creation and Collaboration:

CREATING AND EDITING Documents:

- Document Creation: Starting a new document and selecting templates.
- Editing Tools: Exploring formatting, styling, and text manipulation.

"""

Collaborative Features:

- Real-time Editing: Simultaneous document editing by multiple users.
- Comments and Suggestions: Providing feedback and making collaborative decisions.

11.1.3 Google Sheets: Data Analysis and Management:

CREATING AND FORMATTING Spreadsheets:

- Sheet Creation: Starting a new spreadsheet and organizing data.
- Formatting Tools: Customizing cells, columns, and rows.

Data Entry and Formulas:

- Entering Data: Inputting information into spreadsheets.
- Basic Formulas: Introduction to mathematical and logical functions.

Collaborative Data Analysis:

- Sharing and Editing Spreadsheets: Collaborating on data analysis projects.
- Version History: Tracking changes and reverting to previous versions.

11.1.4 Google Slides: Presentation Development and Collaboration:

CREATING DYNAMIC PRESENTATIONS:

- Slide Creation: Starting a new presentation and choosing themes.

- Adding Content: Inserting text, images, and multimedia elements.

Design and Collaboration:

- Slide Design Options: Customizing the appearance of slides.
- Collaborative Editing: Coordinating with team members in real-time.

11.1.5 Integrations with Other Google Tools:

GOOGLE DRIVE INTEGRATION:

- File Storage and Organization: Managing documents, sheets, and slides in Google Drive.
- Easy Sharing and Access: Simplifying collaboration through shared folders.

11.1.6 Best Practices for Google Docs, Sheets, and Slides:

EFFICIENT DOCUMENT Management:

- Naming Conventions: Establishing a consistent file naming system.
- Folder Organization: Keeping files well-structured for easy retrieval.

Effective Collaboration Strategies:

- Communication within Documents: Using comments and chat for efficient collaboration.
- Setting Permissions: Controlling access levels for document security.

11.1.7 Troubleshooting Common Issues:

DOCUMENT COMPATIBILITY and Version Conflicts:

- Resolving Version Conflicts: Strategies for handling conflicting edits.
- Compatibility with External Software: Ensuring smooth integration with other applications.

11.1.8 Overview of Google Workspace Mobile App:

ACCESSING GOOGLE DOCS, Sheets, and Slides on Mobile Devices:

- Downloading and Installing the Mobile App: Extending Google Workspace capabilities to smartphones and tablets.
- Mobile Features and Functions: Exploring mobile-specific functionalities.

Google Docs, Sheets, and Slides are powerful tools that enhance collaborative work and streamline document creation. As you progress through this course, you will gain practical insights into maximizing the potential of these applications for academic and professional purposes. CIU envisions that this knowledge will empower you to excel in collaborative document creation and effective presentation development. Let's continue this learning journey together!

11.2 Onedrive

WELCOME TO THE MODULE on "Onedrive" at CEPRES International University. In this session, we will explore the capabilities of Onedrive, a cloud storage service that facilitates file management, collaboration, and accessibility. CIU recognizes the importance of efficient file sharing, and this module aims to equip you with the skills needed to effectively use Onedrive for academic and professional purposes.

11.2.1 Introduction to Onedrive:

UNDERSTANDING ONEDRIVE:

- Onedrive is a cloud-based storage solution provided by Microsoft, offering users the ability to store, share, and access files from various devices.
- It is an integral part of Microsoft's suite of productivity tools, enhancing collaboration and accessibility.

11.2.2 Core Features and Functions:

UPLOADING AND ORGANIZING Files:

- File Upload Process: Adding files to Onedrive from different devices.
- Folder Creation and Organization: Structuring files for efficient access.

File Sharing and Collaboration:

- Sharing Files and Folders: Granting access to collaborators.
- Real-time Editing and Collaboration: Simultaneous work on shared documents.

11.2.3 Version Control and Document History:

TRACKING CHANGES AND Versions:

- Version History Overview: Monitoring document changes over time.
- Reverting to Previous Versions: Recovering from undesired

edits.

11.2.4 Accessing Onedrive from Different Devices:

ONEDRIVE ON DESKTOP:

- Installation and Configuration: Setting up Onedrive on a desktop computer.
- Syncing Files: Ensuring offline access and automatic updates.

Onedrive Mobile App:

- Downloading and Installing: Extending Onedrive capabilities to smartphones and tablets.
- Mobile Features and Functions: Accessing and managing files on the go.

11.2.5 Integration with Microsoft 365 Applications:

COLLABORATION WITH Microsoft Word, Excel, and PowerPoint:

- Opening and Editing Documents: Seamless integration with Microsoft Office applications.
- Saving Changes Directly to Onedrive: Streamlining the workflow between applications.

11.2.6 Security and Privacy Considerations:

FILE ENCRYPTION AND Access Controls:

- Ensuring File Security: Encryption methods employed by Onedrive.
- Permission Settings: Controlling who can view or edit files.

11.2.7 Best Practices for Onedrive:

EFFECTIVE FILE NAMING and Organization:

- Naming Conventions: Establishing a consistent file naming system.
- Folder Structure: Organizing files for easy navigation.

Collaborative Strategies:

- Communication within Onedrive: Utilizing comments and chat for efficient collaboration.
- Setting Permissions: Managing access levels for document security.

11.2.8 Troubleshooting Common Issues:

SYNCING PROBLEMS AND Access Issues:

- Basic Troubleshooting Steps: Resolving common technical challenges.
- Onedrive Support Resources: Accessing online support for more complex issues.

11.2.9 Overview of Onedrive Web Interface:

ACCESSING ONEDRIVE through Web Browsers:

- Logging In and Navigating the Interface: Exploring features available on the web interface.
- Advanced Settings and Options: Customizing preferences for a personalized experience.

Onedrive is a powerful tool for cloud storage and collaborative file management. As you progress through this course, you will gain practical insights into maximizing the potential of Onedrive for academic and professional purposes. CIU envisions that this knowledge will empower you to excel in efficient file sharing and management. Let's continue this learning journey together!

233

12 Final Projects and Reflection

12.1 Overview of Final Projects

WELCOME TO THE DISCUSSION on the "Overview of Final Projects" at CEPRES International University. In this session, we will delve into the significance of final projects, how they integrate the skills learned throughout the course, and their role in shaping academic and practical capabilities. CIU emphasizes the importance of practical application, and this discussion aims to provide insights into the purpose and execution of final projects.

12.1.1 Importance of Final Projects:

INTEGRATION OF LEARNED Skills:

- Final projects serve as a culmination of the skills acquired during the course, allowing students to apply theoretical knowledge to real-world scenarios.
- They provide a practical platform for showcasing proficiency in academic success skills, computer skills, and collaborative tools.

Demonstration of Understanding:

- Completing a final project demonstrates a deep understanding of the course content and the ability to synthesize information.
- It allows students to showcase their critical thinking and problem-solving skills.

12.1.2 Collaborative Elements:

TEAM COLLABORATION:

- Many final projects involve collaboration among students, fostering teamwork and communication skills.
- Collaborative tools introduced in the course, such as Google Docs and Onedrive, can be employed for effective teamwork.

Application of Project Management Skills:

- Final projects often require effective project management, including task delegation, timeline adherence, and goal achievement.
- Utilizing project management tools, like Google Sheets, can enhance the efficiency of collaborative efforts.

12.1.3 Diversity of Final Projects:

TAILORED TO COURSE Content:

- Final projects are designed to align with the course objectives and content, ensuring relevance and application.
- They may vary in format, allowing students to choose projects that align with their interests and career goals.

Real-World Application:

- The diversity of final projects mirrors the real-world challenges students may encounter in their academic and professional journeys.
- Addressing practical issues enhances the applicability of the skills learned in the course.

12.1.4 Evaluation and Reflection:

ASSESSMENT CRITERIA:

- Final projects are evaluated based on predefined criteria that assess the application of skills, creativity, and problem-solving.
- This evaluation process provides constructive feedback for continuous improvement.

Reflection on Learning Journey:

- The completion of a final project allows students to reflect on their learning journey, recognizing personal growth and areas for further development.
- CIU. encourages students to introspect on the application of skills beyond the course.

12.1.5 Future Application of Skills Learned:

CAREER READINESS:

- Final projects contribute to students' readiness for future academic pursuits and professional endeavors.
- The skills applied in these projects become valuable assets in various career paths.

12.1.6 Facilitation of Discussion:

SHARING PROJECT EXPERIENCES:

- Participants are encouraged to share their experiences in working on final projects, highlighting challenges, successes, and lessons learned.
- CIU will facilitate the discussion, addressing queries and providing additional insights.

Final projects serve as a transformative phase in the learning journey at CEPRES International University. As we engage in this discussion, let's explore the multifaceted benefits of final projects and how they contribute to the holistic development of each student. CIU envisions that this discussion will inspire a deeper understanding of the role of final projects in shaping academic and professional capabilities. Let the dialogue begin!

12.2 Reflection on the Course

WELCOME TO THE DISCUSSION on "Reflection on the Course" at CEPRES International University. In this session, we will explore the importance of self-reflection as a key component of the learning process CIU encourages students to reflect on their individual progress, the application of learned skills, and the broader implications of the course on their academic and personal journey.

12.2.1 Individual Progress Assessment:

REVIEWING ACADEMIC Success Skills:

- Participants are invited to reflect on the academic success skills covered in the course, including study techniques, time management, goal setting, and note-taking strategies.
- Share personal insights into the effectiveness of these skills in enhancing academic performance.

Application of Computer Skills:

- Reflect on the introduction to basic computer skills, encompassing operating systems, file management, and proficiency in word processing, spreadsheet, and presentation software.
- Discuss personal experiences in applying these skills in

academic and practical settings.

12.2.2 Impact of Collaborative Tools:

UTILIZATION OF COLLABORATION Platforms:

- Explore the use of collaborative tools and project management platforms introduced in the course, such as Google Docs, Sheets, Slides, Onedrive, Microsoft Teams, Zoom, and Google Meet.
- Share instances of successful collaboration and challenges faced in a virtual learning environment.

Final Project Experience:

- Participants are encouraged to reflect on their engagement in the final project, considering the collaborative elements, project management skills, and the application of course content.
- Discuss how the final project contributed to individual growth and the development of teamwork skills.

12.2.3 Lessons Learned and Future Application:

IDENTIFYING KEY TAKEAWAYS:

- Share personal insights into the most significant lessons learned throughout the course, both in terms of skills acquisition and broader perspectives on education.
- Discuss any unexpected discoveries or shifts in thinking.

Future Application of Skills:

- Consider how the skills acquired in this course can be applied in future academic pursuits, professional endeavors, and personal development.

- Explore the potential long-term impact of the course on participants' careers and goals.

12.2.4 Challenges and Overcoming Adversities:

ADDRESSING CHALLENGES:

- Reflect on challenges encountered during the course, whether technical, collaborative, or related to time management.
- Share strategies employed to overcome these challenges and the lessons learned in the process.

12.2.5 Facilitation of Discussion:

OPEN DIALOGUE AND EXCHANGE:

- Participants are encouraged to actively engage in open dialogue, sharing their reflections, posing questions, and responding to peers.
- CIU will facilitate the discussion, offering additional insights and guidance.

As we engage in this reflective discussion, let's collectively explore the individual and collective impact of the course on our academic and personal journeys. CIU envisions that this reflection will contribute to a deeper understanding of the transformative nature of the learning experience at CEPRES International University. Let the reflective dialogue commence!

13.1 Recap of Key Learnings

WELCOME TO THE RECAP session where we will collectively revisit and consolidate the key learnings from the course "Introduction to University Studies" at CEPRES International University. CIU emphasizes the importance of understanding and internalizing these learnings for future academic and professional endeavors.

13.1.1 Academic Success Skills:

EFFECTIVE STUDY TECHNIQUES:

- Participants are encouraged to recap the various study techniques introduced, focusing on their personal preferences and effectiveness.
- Share insights into how these techniques have positively impacted individual study habits.

Time Management Strategies:

- Revisit time management strategies discussed during the course, considering their applicability in balancing academic, personal, and professional commitments.
- Share personal experiences in implementing effective time management.

Goal Setting:

- Recap the importance of goal setting in achieving academic success.
- Discuss personal approaches to goal setting and any

adjustments made throughout the course.

Effective Note-Taking Strategies:

- Explore the different note-taking methods introduced, including digital and traditional approaches.
- Share experiences in using these strategies during lectures and self-study.

13.1.2 Computer Skills and Software Proficiency:

OPERATING SYSTEMS OVERVIEW:

- Recap the fundamentals of various operating systems, including Windows, MacOS, and Linux.
- Share insights into personal preferences and experiences with different operating systems.

File Management Basics:

- Revisit the principles of file management, emphasizing the importance of organized folders and file naming conventions.
- Share personal practices in maintaining a well-organized digital workspace.

Introduction to Productivity Software:

- Recap the basics of word processing, spreadsheet software, and presentation software.
- Discuss personal proficiency in Microsoft Word, Excel, PowerPoint, and other relevant tools.

13.1.3 Internet Skills and Email Communication:

NAVIGATING ONLINE RESOURCES:

- Revisit efficient internet browsing techniques and evaluating online sources.
- Share experiences in conducting online research and identifying reliable resources.

Email Etiquette and Communication:

- Recap the principles of crafting professional emails.
- Share personal insights into maintaining effective email communication.

13.1.4 Video Conferencing Tools and Collaborative Platforms:

INTRODUCTION TO VIDEO Conferencing Tools:

- Recap features and functions of Microsoft Teams, Zoom, and Google Meet.
- Share experiences in participating in virtual meetings and collaborative sessions.

Collaborative Tools and Project Management:

- Revisit the use of Google Docs, Sheets, Slides, and Onedrive for collaboration and project management.
- Discuss the advantages and challenges of working collaboratively in a digital environment.

13.1.5 Final Projects and Reflection:

OVERVIEW OF FINAL PROJECTS:

- Recap the purpose and significance of final projects in applying learned skills.
- Share personal experiences in collaborating on final projects

and the lessons derived.

Reflection on the Course:

- Reflect on the individual progress assessment, challenges faced, and lessons learned throughout the course.
- Share insights into personal growth and the potential long-term impact of the course.

13.1.6 Facilitation of Recap:

OPEN DIALOGUE AND EXCHANGE:

- Participants are encouraged to actively engage in the discussion, sharing their recap insights and learning from peers.
- CIU will facilitate the discussion, offering additional reflections and guidance.

As we recap the key learnings from this course, let's celebrate the collective growth and knowledge gained. CIU envisions that this recap session will solidify the foundation for future academic success and the application of acquired skills. Let the insightful dialogue commence!

13.2 Encouragement for Future Success

WELCOME TO THE DISCUSSION segment where we delve into CIU's encouragement for future success. In this session, participants are invited to reflect on the insights and motivation provided by CIU and share their aspirations for applying these encouragements in their academic and professional journeys.

13.2.1 Reflection on Encouragement:

GRATITUDE AND ACKNOWLEDGMENT:

- Participants are encouraged to express gratitude for CIU.'s guidance and encouragement throughout the course.
- Share specific instances or messages that resonated and motivated you.

Impact on Mindset:

- Reflect on how Dr. Flomo's encouragement has influenced your mindset, particularly in approaching challenges and opportunities.
- Discuss any shifts in perspective or newfound motivation.

13.2.2 Lessons from CEPRES' Formation:

OVERCOMING ADVERSITIES:

- Explore how the challenges faced during the formation of CEPRES, as narrated by Dr. Flomo, serve as lessons in perseverance and determination.
- Discuss personal experiences in overcoming challenges and setbacks.

Strategic Shifts and Adaptability:

- Discuss the importance of strategic shifts in response to challenges and the adaptability showcased in the evolution of CEPRES.
- Reflect on how adaptability can be applied in personal and academic contexts.

13.2.3 Applying Determination and Commitment:

LESSONS IN DETERMINATION:

- Reflect on the determination demonstrated by Dr. Flomo in establishing CEPRES despite initial skepticism.
- Share personal experiences where determination played a crucial role in achieving academic or professional goals.

Time Commitment to Success:

- Discuss the emphasis on time commitment in Dr. Flomo's narrative and how prioritizing time contributes to academic success.
- Share effective time management strategies employed during the course.

13.2.4 Embracing Challenges as Opportunities:

SHIFT IN PERSPECTIVE:

- Explore the concept of viewing challenges as opportunities for growth, as highlighted by Dr. Flomo.
- Share personal experiences where challenges led to valuable learning experiences.

Innovation and Creativity:

- Discuss the innovative approaches taken by Dr. Flomo in responding to challenges, such as partnering with international universities.
- Reflect on the role of innovation and creativity in personal and academic pursuits.

13.2.5 Shaping Future Leaders:

VISION FOR FUTURE LEADERS:

- Explore Dr. Flomo's vision of CEPRES shaping future leaders in environmental and public health.
- Discuss personal aspirations for contributing to positive change and leadership in your chosen field.

13.2.6 Facilitation of Encouragement Exchange:

SHARING ASPIRATIONS:

- Participants are encouraged to share their aspirations for future academic and professional success.

The Lecturer will facilitate the discussion, providing additional insights and encouragement.

As we engage in this discussion on encouragement for future success, let's collectively draw inspiration from Dr. Flomo's journey and share our aspirations for the path ahead. Dr. Flomo envisions that this dialogue will inspire and empower participants to embrace challenges and strive for excellence in their academic and professional pursuits. Let the uplifting conversation begin!

13.3 Additional Resources for Ongoing Learning

IN THIS SEGMENT, WE will explore the importance of continuous learning and discuss additional resources that can further enhance the knowledge gained in the course "Introduction to University Studies" at CEPRES International University. CIU encourages a commitment to ongoing education, and participants are invited to share valuable resources and platforms for continued learning.

13.3.1 Importance of Continuous Learning:

LIFELONG LEARNING MINDSET:

- Discuss the significance of adopting a lifelong learning mindset, as emphasized by Dr. Flomo.
- Share personal perspectives on the role of continuous learning in personal and professional development.

Adapting to Evolving Fields:

- Explore how continuous learning is essential in staying updated and adapting to changes in academic and professional fields.
- Discuss personal experiences where ongoing education has been beneficial.

13.3.2 Types of Additional Resources:

ONLINE COURSES AND Platforms:

- Share recommendations for online learning platforms and courses that complement the skills acquired in the course.
- Discuss the benefits of platforms such as Coursera, edX, or Khan Academy.

Books and Publications:

- Recommend books, articles, or publications that delve deeper into topics covered in the course or related subjects.
- Discuss the impact of reading and scholarly resources on academic growth.

Webinars and Conferences:

- Explore the value of participating in webinars and conferences for gaining insights into emerging trends and research.
- Share experiences attending virtual events and their impact on learning.

13.3.3 Peer Collaboration and Discussion:

ONLINE COMMUNITIES:

- Discuss the benefits of joining online communities or forums related to academic and professional interests.
- Share recommendations for platforms fostering collaboration and knowledge-sharing.

Collaborative Projects:

- Explore the possibility of initiating collaborative projects with peers to apply and expand on the skills learned.
- Discuss the potential for mutual learning through collaborative endeavors.

13.3.4 Guidance and Mentoring:

SEEKING MENTORS:

- Discuss the role of mentors in providing guidance for academic and professional growth.
- Share personal experiences with mentors and the impact on individual development.

Networking Opportunities:

- Explore avenues for networking and connecting with professionals in relevant fields for mentorship and guidance.

- Discuss the benefits of networking in fostering career opportunities.

13.3.5 Facilitation of Resource Exchange:

SHARING VALUABLE RESOURCES:

- Participants are encouraged to share resources they have found valuable for ongoing learning.
- The presenter will facilitate the discussion, offering additional recommendations.

As we explore additional resources for ongoing learning, let's collectively contribute to a pool of valuable recommendations. Dr. Flomo envisions that this discussion will inspire participants to actively seek continuous learning opportunities and leverage diverse resources for their academic and professional journeys. Let the resource-sharing dialogue commence!

14.1 Supplementary Materials

WELCOME TO THE DISCUSSION segment focusing on supplementary materials for the course "Introduction to University Studies" at CEPRES International University. In this session, participants are encouraged to share and discuss additional materials that can enhance understanding, provide further insights, and enrich the learning experience. CIU emphasizes the importance of diverse resources, and participants are invited to contribute to the collective learning journey.

14.1.1 Role of Supplementary Materials:

ENHANCING UNDERSTANDING:

- Discuss how supplementary materials can contribute to a deeper understanding of the course content.
- Share personal experiences where additional resources have clarified complex topics.

Diverse Perspectives:

- Explore the idea that supplementary materials can offer diverse perspectives and enrich the learning experience.
- Discuss the benefits of accessing materials from various authors, institutions, or cultural contexts.

14.1.2 Types of Supplementary Materials:

VIDEO LECTURES AND Documentaries:

- Recommend video lectures or documentaries that align with

the course topics and provide visual insights.

- Discuss the impact of multimedia resources on comprehension.

Podcasts and Audio Resources:

- Share podcasts or audio resources that cover relevant subjects and can be consumed during various activities.
- Discuss the accessibility and flexibility of audio-based learning.

Interactive Simulations and Apps:

- Explore the use of interactive simulations or educational apps that complement the course material.
- Discuss the potential for hands-on learning experiences.

14.1.3 Student-Generated Content:

COLLABORATIVE CONTENT Creation:

- Discuss the idea of students creating and sharing supplementary materials, such as study guides or summary notes.
- Explore platforms for collaborative content creation among peers.

Online Discussion Forums:

- Explore the role of online discussion forums in sharing and discussing supplementary materials.
- Discuss the benefits of collective knowledge-sharing within the student community.

14.1.4 Faculty Recommendations:

GUIDANCE FROM INSTRUCTORS:

- Discuss the impact of faculty-recommended supplementary materials on the learning process.
- Share experiences with instructors providing additional resources for exploration.

Office Hours and Q&A Sessions:

- Explore the potential for utilizing office hours and Q&A sessions to seek guidance on supplementary materials.
- Discuss the importance of open communication with instructors.

14.1.5 Facilitation of Material Exchange:

SHARING PERSONAL RECOMMENDATIONS:

- Participants are encouraged to share supplementary materials they have found valuable.
- The lecturer will facilitate the discussion, offering insights and additional recommendations.

As we delve into the discussion on supplementary materials, let's collectively contribute to a repository of resources that enhance the learning journey. Dr. Flomo envisions that this dialogue will inspire participants to explore a diverse range of materials, fostering a comprehensive understanding of university studies. Let the exchange of supplementary materials commence!

. . . .

14.2 Glossary of Terms

WELCOME TO THE DISCUSSION on creating a glossary of terms for the course "Introduction to University Studies" at CEPRES International University. In this session, participants are encouraged to collaborate in identifying key terms, concepts, and terminology relevant to the course content. CIU emphasizes the importance of clarity in language, and the goal is to create a comprehensive glossary for mutual understanding.

14.2.1 Importance of a Glossary:

ENHANCING COMMUNICATION:

- Discuss how a glossary contributes to clear communication and comprehension within the academic context.
- Share instances where a well-defined glossary has improved understanding.

Standardizing Terminology:

- Explore the role of a glossary in standardizing terminology across various topics covered in the course.
- Discuss the benefits of consistency in language usage.

14.2.2 Identification of Key Terms:

COURSE-SPECIFIC TERMS:

- Participants are invited to identify terms specific to "Introduction to University Studies" that may require definition.
- Discuss the importance of understanding course-specific terminology.

Academic and Technical Language:

- Explore academic and technical language used in the course content that might be unfamiliar to some participants.
- Share experiences of encountering academic jargon and its impact on learning.

14.2.3 Collaborative Definition Creation:

DEFINING KEY TERMS:

- Participants can collaboratively create concise and clear definitions for identified key terms.
- Discuss the importance of creating definitions that are accessible to all students, regardless of their background.

Incorporating Examples:

- Explore the inclusion of examples or contextual explanations to enhance the understanding of each term.
- Discuss how real-world examples can aid in grasping abstract concepts.

14.2.4 Accessibility and Format:

ACCESSIBLE FORMAT:

- Discuss the preferred format for presenting the glossary to ensure accessibility for all students.
- Explore the possibility of creating both digital and printable versions.

Integration with Course Material:

- Explore ways to integrate the glossary with course materials,

making it easily accessible during study sessions.
- Discuss the potential for an interactive digital glossary.

14.2.5 Facilitation of Collaboration:

SHARING CONTRIBUTIONS:

- Participants are encouraged to share their contributions to the glossary.
- The lecturer will facilitate the discussion, offering insights and guiding the collaborative definition process.

As we engage in creating a glossary of terms, let's collectively contribute to a resource that enhances understanding and fosters a shared language within the academic community. Dr. Flomo envisions that this collaborative effort will result in a valuable tool for students embarking on their university studies. Let the definition crafting begin!

14.2.6 Review and Refinement:

PEER REVIEW:

- Participants can engage in a peer review process, providing feedback on definitions created by their peers.
- Discuss the benefits of collaborative review in ensuring accuracy and clarity.

Feedback Incorporation:

- Explore how feedback received can be incorporated into the glossary to improve the quality of definitions.
- Discuss the importance of an iterative process in glossary development.

14.2.7 Implementation in Learning:

INTEGRATION INTO COURSE Modules:

- Discuss how the glossary can be seamlessly integrated into different course modules for easy reference.
- Explore the potential for linking specific terms to relevant sections in course materials.

Interactive Learning Activities:

- Explore the possibility of incorporating interactive learning activities that involve the use of the glossary.
- Discuss how such activities can reinforce the understanding of key terms.

14.2.8 Inclusivity and Accessibility:

MULTILINGUAL CONSIDERATIONS:

- Participants are encouraged to consider the inclusivity of the glossary, especially for students with diverse language backgrounds.
- Discuss strategies for ensuring that the glossary accommodates multilingual needs.

Accessibility Features:

- Explore the incorporation of accessibility features in the glossary, such as alternative text for visual elements.
- Discuss ways to make the glossary accessible to students with varying learning needs.

14.2.9 Ongoing Maintenance:

RESPONSIBILITY FOR Updates:

- Discuss how the glossary will be maintained and updated as new terms emerge or as course content evolves.
- Explore the possibility of involving students in the ongoing maintenance process.

Feedback Mechanisms:

- Establish feedback mechanisms for students to suggest new terms or revisions to existing definitions.
- Discuss the importance of creating a dynamic and responsive glossary.

As we conclude this discussion on the glossary of terms, let's celebrate the collaborative effort in creating a valuable resource for the course. CIU expresses gratitude for the commitment to fostering a shared understanding and language within the academic community. The glossary is now ready to serve as a beacon of clarity and accessibility for all students embarking on their university studies journey. Let the enriched learning experience begin!

· · · ·

14.3 Bibliography

ABOUT-OUR-ACCREDITED-online-university-texila-american-university. (n.d.). Tauedu. Retrieved January 20, 2024, from https://tauedu.org/about-us/

Allen, D. (2003). Getting Things Done: The Art of Stress-Free Productivity. Penguin.

Bandura, A. (1991). Social cognitive theory of self-regulation. Organizational Behavior and Human Decision Processes, 50(2), 248–287.

Barkley, E. F., Cross, K. P., & Major, C. H. (2014). Collaborative Learning Techniques: A Handbook for College Faculty. John Wiley & Sons.

Buzan, T. (1996). The Mind Map Book: Unlock your creativity, boost your memory, change your life. BBC Active.

CEPRES Journal of Science and Innovative Studies. (n.d.). Retrieved January 20, 2024, from https://cepresjournal.org/

Chick, N. L., & Watson, G. (2002). Creating a Learning Society: A New Approach to Growth, Development, and Social Progress. Johns Hopkins University Press.

Cirillo, F. (2018). The Pomodoro Technique. Currency.

components of operating system image—Google Search. (n.d.). Retrieved January 19, 2024, from https://www.google.com/search?q=components+of+operating+system+image&oq=components+o

Covey, S. R. (1989). The 7 Habits of Highly Effective People. Free Press.

Covey, S. R. (1994). First Things First. Simon and Schuster.

Deci, E. L., & Ryan, R. M. (2000). The "what" and "why" of goal pursuits: Human needs and the self-determination of behavior. Psychological Inquiry, 11(4), 227–268.

Doran, G. T. (1981). There's a S.M.A.R.T. way to write management's goals and objectives. Management Review, 70(11), 35–36.

Dweck, C. S. (2017). Mindset: The New Psychology of Success. Random House.

Emmons, R. A. (1996). Striving for the sacred: Personal goals, life meaning, and religion. Journal of Social Issues, 51(2), 73–90.

Friel, J., & Friel, L. (2011). The 7 Habits of Highly Effective Teens Workbook. Touchstone.

Goodier, B., & Sorger, C. (2013). Evernote for Dummies. John Wiley & Sons.

Google Scholar. (n.d.). Retrieved January 18, 2024, from https://scholar.google.com/

google slides images—Google Search. (n.d.). Retrieved January 20, 2024, from https://www.google.com/ search?q=google+slides++images&sca_esv

Hyerle, D. (2000). Thinking Maps: Visual Tools for Activating Habits of Mind. ASCD.

IAMA – IAMA. (n.d.). Retrieved January 20, 2024, from https://iama-india.org/

Klosowski, T. (2019). Lifehacker: The Guide to Working Smarter, Faster, and Better. Wiley.

Lincoln University College | Top Private University Degree & Medical College In Malaysia. (n.d.). Retrieved January 20, 2024, from https://lincoln.edu.my/

Locke, E. A., & Latham, G. P. (2002). Building a practically useful theory of goal setting and task motivation: A 35-year odyssey. American Psychologist, 57(9), 705–717.

Locke, E. A., & Latham, G. P. (2002). Building a practically useful theory of goal setting and task motivation: A 35-year odyssey. American Psychologist, 57(9), 705–717.

McKeachie, W. J., Svinicki, M. D., & Hofer, B. K. (2006). McKeachie's Teaching Tips: Strategies, Research, and Theory for College and University Teachers. Cengage Learning.

McMillan, K., & Weyers, J. (2015). How to Write Essays & Assignments. Pearson UK.

Microsoft word images free—Google Search. (n.d.).

Nilson, L. B. (2010). Teaching at Its Best: A Research-Based Resource for College Instructors. John Wiley & Sons.

Pauk, W. (2013). How to Study in College. Cengage Learning.

Pauk, W., & Owens, R. (2015). How to Study in College. Cengage Learning.

Prochaska, J. O., Norcross, J. C., & DiClemente, C. C. (1994). Changing for Good. William Morrow Paperbacks.

ResearchGate | Find and share research. (n.d.). ResearchGate. Retrieved January 18, 2024, from https://www.researchgate.net/

Ruscio, J. (2006). Clear Thinking with Psychology: Separating Sense from Nonsense. Cengage Learning.

Ruscio, J. (2018). A Student's Guide to Academic Success. Macmillan Learning.

Sharda University—A Truly Global University. (n.d.). Retrieved January 20, 2024, from https://www.sharda.ac.in/URL

Smith, A. M., & Smith, P. (2016). Reading to Learn in a Writing Classroom. In M. Soven (Ed.), Writing Spaces: Readings on Writing (Vol. 2). Parlor Press.

Smith, M. K. (2002). The Advantages of Charting. Retrieved from http://www.infed.org/biblio/b-chart.htm

Top real estate and construction management Institute in India| 1000+ Alumni's. (n.d.). IREF. Retrieved January 20, 2024, from https://iref.co.in/

Tracy, B. (2014). Eat That Frog!: 21 Great Ways to Stop Procrastinating and Get More Done in Less Time. Berrett-Koehler Publishers.

Vanderkam, L. (2016). 168 Hours: You Have More Time Than You Think. Penguin.

Willingham, D. T. (2017). The Reading Mind: A Cognitive Approach to Understanding How the Mind Reads. John Wiley & Sons.

Zotero | Downloads. (n.d.). Retrieved January 21, 2024, from https://www.zotero.org/download/

About the Author

Dr. Mogana S. Flomo, Jr., born in 1976 in Liberia, is a prominent figure in academia, agriculture, and public health. As Founder of CEPRES Inc. and CEPRES International University, he champions education, environmental sustainability, and public health. With 26 years in academia, he serves as a lecturer and consultant, shaping higher education in Liberia. Notably, he led Liberia's agricultural sector as the Former Minister of Agriculture, advocating for sustainability and smallholder farmers empowerment. Dr. Flomo's entrepreneurial endeavors focus on innovative strategies for smallholder farmers. A prolific author, he contributes significantly to literature in agriculture, environmental sustainability, Education, and public health. Board memberships further showcase his commitment to holistic development, leaving an indelible mark on Liberia's progress.

www.ingramcontent.com/pod-product-compliance
Lightning Source LLC
Chambersburg PA
CBHW050503160726
48003CB00001B/133